CALLS

Robert Kelly

a word purifies itself in being spoken—

lift the sky off
just once to see
the imageless other

ourselves the sea

Lunar Chandelier Collective

Lunar Chandelier Collective
Catskill, New York
(a subset of Lunar Chandelier Press)

lunarchandeliercollective@gmail.com
http://lunarchandelier.blogspot.com

First Edition.

ISBN: 978-0-9997831-0-8

Cover text, layout and design by Terrence Arjoon
Interior text typset in Iowan Old Style

for Charlotte
beloved
who gave me the island
and gave me the sea

CALLS

1.
Trees don't walk
hylonoetic manifesto
a word you won't find

in dictionaries
they don't want you to know
trees talk

trees think in us
that's how they get around
we speak their mind

as we near them
each thing speaks its own
dialect of thought

the manyness of them
at work in us
signs from afar

that reach us,
teach us, the long
sermon of a stick of wood.

2.
The calls are causes
listen to me
three times round the island

and stay your hand
no one is guilty
only the gull can look down on us

angustia that narrow thing
angina, a squeeze, *anguis,* a snake,
anxiety the coil of worry

round the moment when
every stroke of time wants to be free.
Be me (I wanted to tell her)

be me looking at you,
watching the slither of your absence
the panoply of human evidence

but these are fancies
bred of remembering too well
what I should never have seen in the first place

now I am a slave to what I observed.
Serve it, serve
the imaginary perceiving we call real.

3.
Every wall has a door in it
waiting for the door
not easy to find

every wind has a door in it
every air
or open the light and go through

it is all about doors today
the number three
the in the out and the between

daleth a door they say is four
I counted three
for *aleph* is zero, what has never been said.

4.
Ice was. And then.
Refrigeration. Engineering
grandfather. Great circle.

We are here on the boat,
boat on water, water on planet
the boat goes round.

There are religious reasons for everything
the serious tone of local conversations.
"Thoughtful" was a word I overheard.

Lighthouse lovers estuaries
youthful voices of old men.
community a kind of song,

living out loud all
the special anxieties of music
among the animates.

5.
The sea
comes in three.
Analogy of breath.

In, pause, out,
om ah hum,
the foundation,

trinity basic to life systems
from which every
trinity arises,

and three
is the first number,
before it only

a woman standing on the beach
alone, from the waves
a man crawls out onto land

dares to stand
beside her
and the numbers start.

6.
Three, the sea.
Osprey over Canapitsit
unknown into the unknown.

This is theology coming
thought's superstar
a little long in the tooth

Dietrich in the elevator at MoMA
remembrances of the Great War
every day, love of a lady

the sea is all about capacity
to come and come and do it again,
the shore trembles at your suit

the writing man,
he hath three hands
what I have seen defines me

does a word come with it
halogen the old French air
bathing suit abandoned on the beach

photograph the absence
sound of wine gurgling in goblet
the white wall of sad young men

song please of the empty carton
folded rather briskly
caressed by clerkly hands

and vacant, poignant, pregnant
with all the words that mean
I have come to you, my lad.

7.
The first day here is a ferry to myself
the course leads by the sirens' conversation
into the evidence of actual place

to walk there, to understand
liberty is a function of number
a kind of prime you know by feel

Galois in his sleeping cap,
instinct is not enough for counting
we need silence too —

so the space between your integers,
your lips, the sway of certainty
before the dance of negative numbers

what *is* he talking about now
the look of things and places
when you say a, lay a, prayer upon them.

8.
Overlay of compassion
through the dream of which
you can see crowded streets

or lonely trees, and your mother
reading by the mountain lake
or anything at all, take

comfort from the mantra
moaned over the mere moon
your cold unborn brother

Paulownia, my princess permission
those fragrant purple flowers
before any common leaf

or pick a rapture of your own
inconsequential miracles of love
we wake from just soon enough

to keep the empire running
of our half acre if that, counting
no higher than our fingers.

9.
Morning noble cloud arrival
windows getting ready
exhaustion has a way with words

run out of meanings
clouds alive us
I swear it on the sea glare

the light out there looks like mind
herself shining on calm tide
air is land is shadow

to say the name all new
or be out of language
boatless the shore

I have been waiting
so long for again
but again never comes

and so the startlement happens
a bare patch on the lawn
who knows what seeds will

and even if they do
who is their mother?
So welcome those blue flowers

for her sake, and Rilke's sake,
and all the distances you once breathed in
before the lamina of doubt deposited

and doubt is the same as getting old —
a miracle is a thing to look at and believe
learn from the experience of love

I don't know it's one thing
it could be many
water droplets make one cloud

or coming later, the way a possum
comes out back home beneath the moon
big over Gayhead in the sixth month cool.

10.
Cluster of beginnings
milk as ink
translation from the Slavic

leg wrapped round the pole
Munsee legends thorn-pig up the tree
lily athlete relent relent

we all are flowers only,
osprey over channel
twice a week the mail comes in

but never news of you
who live inside me anyway
marshaling what passes as my thought

who but desire could assemble so many
in architecture and dialect
teasing out the divine

nature of it, they
used to build a dome above it
but we are naked now.

11.
 am on another planet
a traveling company of actors
singing *Don Giovanni* — the music is familiar

everything else is strange.
I am strange. This is called sleep,
being asleep, a different planet,

a different music always the same.
Il mio tesoro he sings, McCormack
a century ago,

sixty-four notes on one breath
the war almost over.
There is a blue sun

around which this world turns
their sky is like our sea,
their flesh like our flesh.

12.
So all these things are waiting
to turn into miracles the minute
you turn and look at them

the coast of Latvia, the smell
of yesterday's paulownia flower
faint as last year's Honolulu lei

I cant help it, love is terror,
a far-off contralto singing French,
what can any human do but listen

and what is listening
but the ear-womb yearning to conceive—
for every one of us must give birth

you can't leave all that work to women
and the waves sweep gently in today
reminding us of everywhere else.

13.
Road against the light
à beau lire le hasard
no chance at all but circumstance

what stands around me
spoke after sunrise
flocculent clouds teasing horizon

pens in their glass on the windowsill my flowers
this flock of sheep my waking
but it's you who count in this histoire

turbulence and small republics
no bigger than my living room
and ruled by you of course of nature

Being, through the glare
the little animal *contra mundum*
silly truth that things are sentient

things think in us how else would we,
I wouldn't call it philosophy
a sparrow with an eagle in its clutches.

14.
The order in which things come to mind
all things carouse in aspiration
the trumpet clinks against the trombone's bell

it doesn't need me to make noise
for it is talking all the time
one bedroom after another

until the king gives birth to the queen
will is just another consequence of cause
my Spinoza would begin that way

demur demission sit by your window
and pass the world slowly before your eyes
until joy beats down the door and lets you in.

15.
Unspeakable resemblances in the clouds
Polonius died from visions he feared to tell,
we are unhinged by what we do not speak

that should be clear by now
fisher folk not staring into glare
oh children of desire hide in the light!

Who knows what happens it begins again
René Goupil murdered by Mohawks
he is close today, a forgiving agency

and some mornings demons attack
crawling up the nervous system
the only place where they can operate

the optick Nerve eroded and chew'd through
so that I see through Dusk at Noone
a glimmer of far island hope

it takes a long time to hear the trees
but then the wood sings, all matter sings,
signs, says, means, minds.

All we can do is know in them
I don't know where the Other came from
it keeps me living aqua viva

to whom we pray lackadaisical
hump of day, cloud sprinkle, sage
comfort and a blackbird believe you

bayberry tree older than to see
waxy fragrance gateway to mind's palazzo
where the wedding march actually goes.

16.
I owe you a letter
let it be aleph
and you be Beth

reading me
on your young camel
while I wait in the doorway

I am the door, he said,
and we are his house.
he let us in, let us be, his word

any word knows how to do that,
be the entrance and the entered thing at once,
and lovers almost hand in hand

saunter in, pretend to look around
but really searching for the holy
temple of any empty room.

17.
There's a sky up there
and over that an empty space
some days, a spear or two of light

but mostly silence.
We are the air.
We never understand,

birds imagine us,
they picture us as angels,
all of us messengers

who have forgotten our message
if we ever had one—
what *did* that mountain say?

18.
Time to let the dragons speak
they have a right to clarity
Pound's *ming* in the second tone, its homophones,

why is clarity like having a name
for everything you meet, a name
to offer strangers as your own

b'midbar in the wilderness
which is also the wordlessness
since all your language comes from trees

Eden book *Buchstabe* birch bark
the final dragon is the name of things,
a book is the cave he's hoarding in

but he does not come from there
draco hominis spiraculum
a dragon is the human breath

this primal cave my thorax
its mouth my mouth he said
then Shakespeare slept, who taught us all we know.

19.
Sun and moon sleeping together
men and women naked in space
walk this cosmic gulf we call the Earth

the gender of genius is a dragon's doubt
a lion's skeptic mouth
how long since I have bitten thee

yes, breath — his famous fire is my simple breath
his flapping wings my bones,
thighbone trumpet, backbone scale

the twelve-tone music of the dormant mind
up the ladder, little mouse,
wake the muse all sultry up below

you touch the bottom from the top
and all things operate by opposites
sea would drown us though we come from sea

home is never a place to go back to
silly humans with their scuba gills,
be true to source by flowing from.

20.
No grief like the grief of words
Moses on the mountain heard a voice
turned hearing into commandment

who can this man of Egypt be
whose face afflicts us with the leprosy of law
what is this clarity that is too clear

we worship clouds because they come and go
veins of the sky we say
or words and cries of shaman priests

set afloat above an innocent planet
still learning to control a central fire
our indoor oceans, our habit of life

not all places are alive but all places think
universal sentience is a scandal
like a gorgeous opera that never ends.

21.
We visited Verona tomb of Juliet
heard her still breathing past the stone
the trains were late that day and autumn early

it's your dance to make all the connections
no authorities in your thinking help
you can be any place you hear

and you can play in wisdom and in pleasure there
that is the promise of poetry
from which Aeneas tried all his life to hide

why build a city? To hide language in
so all the words get said at once
and no one listens and everything begins.

Moses too bright to look at
because he had seen the hinder parts of God
since no one sees the face of God and lives

achorei on that mountain
we should only see each other from behind
the body tells the truth the face dissembles

any lover knows that in his sleep
there is gloom of knowing too much
folly of trusting what you know

eat your breakfast and set to work
the only truth is what happens
he hid his face so none could see his grief

for no man can look on sorrow and survive
our faces teach us feeling, and feelings kill —
empathy, black hole of other people.

22.
Mourning dove's slow tone becomes
a church bell far
Sundays me to wake

where is the temple now?
Where are all the Masses said
on whose bare skin or grasslands gone

grabbed from the First Nations
when the real first nation was the word
that noise we heard

spent millennia interpreting
till now I tell you what it means
comrade sister all things are alive

the same as you are living
in the desert of the word
slopes of the same barren mountain

he said but we didn't believe him
poetry is drama anyhow
each line its sole protagonist

and like opera they all die at the end
leave us with the taste of truth
salty in the open wound we call a mouth.

23.
Grim as a flag on a bright day
gaiety of war
and no one ever remembers

we are monsters we live forever
no wars are ever won or ever done
the end result is always money

nations tricked by men to act like men
killing, killing "to feed the moon"   *GIG*
he said but we knew better

what would church be like if it came to us
or maybe the sound of bells is enough
transubstantiation of the air itself

relationship of *interior prayer* to public war
no such thing as conscience cries the State
despises that Spinoza stuff the ethical

how could we live without our sickness
would we not be open-minded to the sunlight
this island almost a stateless society

what does a soldier think
in that soul of theirs "love might one day rise"   *TM*
and that would be the end of war

inside every photo is a demon's face
who told you so? He did — did you believe him?
Who else is there to believe

who else has looked so deeply
into the images by which we try to tell the truth
the signs in which we think?

30

24.
The elm tree calls and the widow's walk,
sea bass on steeple of the mer-folk's church
a million religions in any minute

listen, this is gospel he kept insisting
not just insights from Spinoza
of course the world's what's left of God

or what we see when God passes by
and unmanacles our eyes and lo!
the ordinary animal of earth, the us.

25.
Simple as a mother speaking
"Some things that go are gone"   *ARA*
the things are gone, the world is here

could that ever be enough
a sonnet of broken bottles
a statue made of straw?

I want to sound like someone else today
so the witches won't catch me,
they'll think some Frenchman's talking

big about identity and self
while all the while the little boy
rolls a red rubber ball along the leg of a little girl

and the moon is full of rabbits
and the apple tree is in blossom in the snow
animals masquerading as my friends

touch the stone
it all comes better then,
you forget the massacres,

the ballpoint pens like fingers
reaching out to claw you, forget
and remember the silky suchness of the stone

green one she picked up by the Barges
and said This will hold your words in place
before the wild sun sweeps everything away.

26.
Call is all is *kol* is caul
the sound a meaning comes wrapped in as it's born
look over there a deer browsing

danger everywhere of making sense
sense calls from every burning bush
sense calls from every bush awake or sleeping

sense calls from every bird, every rail it lands on
sense calls from everything you see or hear
sense calls from silence.

27.
It's all religion really
an island is all religion
America Great Turtle Island

ocean enforces natural piety
would I have spoken if no one called
or is it me always calling into silence

words imply a hearer
to call implies someone called
to call out implies a God

*gaudh-, 'what is called out to'
defining that unknown by all
we know about her, it is she to whom we call.

28.
What was my original name?
Something with blue flowers
a glacier, crevasse in sunlight

window of a wooden house
something red. Red.
Snow falling on the opera house

as if the music never stops —
but I know there was another name
a steel box welded shut

a snake beneath the Virgin's heel.
We belong to images
but will any image tell me my true name?

29.
When a child was a wishing well
he could be anything he saw
grew tall from pine trees by the Delaware

became continuous because a river was,
is, child, amalgam, ambix, athanor
— never grow up! — the heart is true

is made of something like ivory
brain in a bone, curtain of silk
trembling while the actors take their places

we need sciences only partway right
our lovelorn errors crave a simpler world
listen, a myth is waking up

you hear it breathing in your chest
its pulse is in the back of your head
we mostly need the world behind us

seed scattered on a beach in vain
where Augustine fitted the ocean into his little pail
oh every story has two ends

turn it backwards to tell the truth
simplicity profound —
we think because we can sit down.

30.
Problems of faith what happens
when your friend wears a shirt like that
he is not your friend says the dream

how can I tell what the dream said from what I think
isn't there a muscle in the mind
something that knows its own strength and says so

or is it always a room full of women
muses, bacchantes, slim-skirted editors?
No, these women are poets and painters and prophets

scientists of the unknowable
the part of me I love more than myself
pilgrims in an illuminating dream

all philosophy is a knot in a pine wood plank
but what is the rest of that pale matter,
resinous, softer, continuous?

31.
We don't call them that anymore
we call them paradigms or syntax
even when they wear alluring clothes

because everything is changed here
starting of course with the names
names are the places between things

rescue me like a road
clouds know everything how can I listen
to those islands overhead

to be so terribly orphan late
when no one cares a car drives on
why do I have to know the things I know

offload memory into empery
you rule the world when you've forgotten everything
that's where the black car is going

the fire drill, the yellow bus all forgotten
the King of Spain hides in his tomb
last chords of *Parsifal* in French

you can tell who listens by a pain in the chest
air-sack, blood pump, clogged tubes,
rusty chassis, thorax full of noise.

32.
It makes you wonder
and a wonder you remain
skin like ivory no dare had touched

the wave calls and why
life comes after something else
don't we know that even yet, that we are *from?*

Everything clear around me I am not clear
Why is resilience like a battered trumpet?
Where does the river sleep?

The trumpet shall sound but we were not sleeping
language kept vigil for us as we drowsed
I heard a little bell where there is no air

no sound in a vacuum
island always on horizon
catboat with its sail down

take a cab to me and chew through the door
show the undercroft to distinguished visitors
yes I will be your bishop you my saint

we are sick with adjectives
let us be naked in the mountain air
no one is watching the moon is blind

but what if the sky itself is full of signs
for whom have we been acting all these years
the script I improvise with such effort

we forgive anything but relevance —
no numbers please — things just go on
warm but wind, mist on horizon.

33.
At her rising, Hesht, through the planes
spoken in the afterlife, Osiris, Ansar us!
On the first day there are big waves

men doubt their mothers all their lives
teach me fractions, let me taste the chalk
write me the story of me loving you

get it right on your side true forever
men like noise women like quiet
men like machines for making noise

and war is the biggest machine of all
a gist of gender
a toxoplasmic parasite in the male brain

just watch the woman striding down the street
disperse armies in the desirous night
noctilucent girlfriends on the edge of sleep

the wind is talking again
it makes my mind up for me
wing whir! Bird out of mist! What name?

Help the sun shine help the osprey fly
turn a glad face up to Lady Sun
talk to people's backs their innocent flesh

when all the letters have been sent
the sky unzips and a new face peeks out
dream dome you saw just once before

the celadon is rising
I hate the moon
he's mean to the meaning of me in her.

34.
Is it after all the name of a man
just a sound you make
softly when you're alone?

Try another keyboard
this one just makes tones
tones make no sense

but that's just what I don't want to make
to call is to forgive.
To call is to care.

I want the one that has you in it
to feel reverence for the other side of life
once upon a time there was no death

people grew too crowded at the river
not enough food too many old too many young
so someone had the bright idea of dying

everybody chose one man to do the killing
and called him Death or was it a woman —
the ones he or she comes for never tell —

a sad and painful job she has, or he,
but they let him live forever
painless and crying, hurt only by grief,

sustained by compassion and philosophy
she is invisible, or he is, and has to be
lest one day she see himself in a mirror

for none can look on me and live
she said and then I woke intelligent
at last in this matter that concerns us all

vainly since we can't help or mar her
or would you rather be killed by a man
your choice, just close your eyes.

35.
Bravery slavery words are always trying to tell
us something we don't want to know
but language purifies itself in speaking

as my father told me rivers do in running
leaving all silt behind, a deposit of evidence
from which only poetry and revelation grow

Lutetia the muddy place city of light
heart of alchemy tower of St. James
from drekh we prophesy and make our gold

not so different from yours but lasts forever
byang-chub, liberation, enlightenment totally clear
have I not tasted this water once before

I wasn't ready to begin
it came upon me as I slept
I don't answer but your questions make me strong.

36.
The call. Why do they call?
Rilke's *Lockruf*, things also
call out to us from where they are

so close to us in a single world.
Dove afternoon, plaint comes like a breeze,
he is calling to his mate, his love, his muse?

There is an animal in me that knows how to talk
Thinglish is the language he deposes,
and I tend to trust to him more than the rest of me

or the towhee in the elm tree's drink-your-tea —
for once I am obedient
sipping Assam my true love brought me

so it's all like a folk song
after all, however much we spend
that's all we'll ever be

inheritors of music, our only choice the scale
the so-called key
to no door anywhere

except as Strauss said — his brain
organized by key signature,
except as the wind says, it's always in Me Major.

37.
Don't write about the sea today
the sea is tired of your lyric
it wants a narrative of flesh and iron

or that's what the waves said at Church's Beach
he can't throw a tower down
unless he comes with hero in his heart.

38.
I sleep the way others drink
sleep itself is universal drunkenness
for consciousness to lose itself

when every day we grow so
conscious of ourselves in everything
but aware of nothing

can it be that awareness "one day will rise"   *TM*
and the false claims of consciousness be stilled?
To be conscious is to be me, to be aware is just to be.

Is that to say too much to say?
An animal moving in the dark outside
coyote maybe, leftover wisdom, not much moon

I will write until the sun comes up
and that will be enough of me
it is the body that instructs us in all arts

the body is Prometheus or
art is the eagle feeds on our insides,
in us alone the sun must rise.

39.
Wake in the dark to analyze the light
dry island mirror of a stateless nation
we're all born together what else can we do or go

we are the language
life makes us for itself
to be more and always more

and if more than one sun came up today
what then, Coleridge, in your golden flower,
can't life wake and not be me

be a part of morning like the dove
its call already heard
at the sky's first hint of light?

but light is some other island
across the channel from where we live
nothing native in nature

it's all imported from afar—
all human skills are from Prometheus
the one who thought before the world

his raven comes to us and cries our way along
we only have to follow what we hear
when no one's speaking.

40.
The whale needs the sea
but does the sea need the whale
does the earth need me

'me' is an algebraic term
it has no special mother
girlfriends everywhere, or boys depending

ten thousand years who will remember this
we always find a good way to forget
leave every song unfinished

I watched the dawn, no splendor
just a gentle crayoning of light
from east to south, then sky a pearl bedded over us

let the stone remember
we have other work to do
light waking over our little islands.

So much for religion
now the rights of women,
what we owe to God.

41.
A finch on a feeder
what fun is that
to a wifeless wind in an empty moon

tells us no one is ever alone,
the language goes on
language is always somebody else

and if the wind died down
who would I even be
calls them his 'issues'

though issue means pus from a sore
a newspaper full of lies
blood seeping from the inmost chalice.

42.
How could there be a wrong number
the little girl asked, Pythagoras already,
it's men who are wrong

women silent downstream in a kayak
could this be love?
Shadows of tall buildings on the water

the wind is wild the sea is calm
each animal keeps its own heart close
safe from language as can be

all Delius on the radio deep green breeze
Strauss born today, his head in Salome's lap,
music gets above itself and rules the world.

43.
Dawn again the Don of sleep has left his Doña
to run about again, constant energy
you know those exiles

this whole day is a foreign country
will I ever learn its speech
I want to build a world already there

who can blame the crow for calling
to the trained ear his caw is grammatical
the real language I yearn to know

calls out lucidly to the heart
so a child learns to comprehend
clearer than uncles and aunts

those dragons in weird-smell houses
loud pianos scorching radiators
ants on floorboards no one you recognize.

44.
Language had saved me from myself
to my surprise it was almost morning
we walked by the long meadow

side by side like shadows of each other
you can hear the tone of it already
blind Delius over the hill

where had we gone and who had we been
every now and then we saw the clouds
the sun was a distracted thinker

mostly we thought road and dog a farm away
and for all I know we still are walking
the footage of memory unspools in the closet

there could be no magic without the ordinary
in which it hides, its surface
common as coffee or a hammer

but its nails are made of light
and that cup is made of consciousness
and memory unmakes the mind

magic always needs a place to hide
why not here among the chalks and pencils
where tiny humans learn long words

even 'truth' the longest word of all
write with a pen you can stick in your pocket
you taste when you lick your fingers.

45.

The Prophet's Song

Will I ever be
the other side of me

will the birds I praise
answer me at last

and when I speak
will forests listen?

Or is it people, people
all the time

but all the rocks and rills
have already heard too much ?

46.
Laugh me a jigsaw
I can work on through the night
to show my own face by morning

learning not to pay attention
think about a steamboat on the river
full of naked gamblers

with nothing to stake but the time of their lives
and from the levees townsfolk watch
sweating in their Sunday clothes

call this America and vote against it
at all the polling stations of the heart
where money changes into things to eat

work in the morning worry, sun hazy
sea bright all the way to Santiago
the grail is hidden there in family matters

revoked the Bible flew to the moon
stayed three nights, came back, flew to the sun
and speaks to us from her insistent light

end of story the rest is hierarchy
sit at the window and bless the procession
the whole world loves to pass you by.

47.
Being is such an ordeal
in a place in particular
such hard work being alive

the edges of experience are painful
time to be forgotten
behind your back is where the action is

that's why nobody lives in the sky
except the swallows over Sade's château
contra naturam and very beautiful

allow me the adverb, it's afternoon and innocent
you detect me at my work
trying to make sense out of nothing

am I an ocean with no water or with no shore
try to keep your body to yourself
what a bird flies up for and never finds

I am named after Chinese poetry she said
her sweet Baltic accent hard to follow in Berlin
I am a kind of sea fog with an opera in it

people keep understanding themselves —
just keep talking the truth comes out
we live here to look at the sea our mother

I wonder does she even remember us
she has so many children some still at home
but we have gone into the west, into the flesh

so far from Ireland, Devon, Picardy
genetic heartlands of humble heart
bent on listening to the waves and nothing more

we walked by the Defense Canal
then watched the trains come in and not go out
the huge sky fitted round her face

one more mystery among so many
and I knew that once again museum feeling
I could possess this person and never touch.

48.
Setting the mind at ease is worth a Mass
he said, mist still on the foreland
what will come or what will call

I heard her voice speaking from the ground
phosphorescent rocks sent my question
I owe you a letter let's call it *yod*

a hand a stem cell a tear a bead of sweat
let's call it Roundtop in the Blues
where my ruined wisdom temple gapes

come play in me every body calls
sol et luna amplex'd in the bone
worry quiet whistle in the wood

tall-finned sea bass throng local waters
my body also made of you
eating be all thank-you and forgive-me

I found that carved on Sinai shards
a man's face is always yesterday —
describe only places you have never been.

49.
Are you ready for the everything again
imagine having to memorize the world
(that's what language does)

I have a theory of visual art
here's how to begin your painting
breathe on the mirror

the world alas is full of mirrors
the world is drowning in wisdom
sad queens afloat in asses' milk

sit on the ground and eat what you find
we have to begin again again
wind yearns for your artful sails

we're always going back to pick things up
this buttercup alone where sand paths intersect
music is old the minute it is heard

that's why it sells so well and poetry so poorly
since language is always new
no matter how many times you hear it

how would we look without mirrors
my father's back at ninety clear and fresh—
a muscle of guessing torques us onward.

50.
This is my *Clarel* with no clear Holy Land
yet every footstep makes an island
and every island is a Palestine

where I can call myself a Jew at last
and claim you for my *minyan*
so we can pray the alphabet together.

51.
Flame advances next town over
sad dusty shop front like British Legion
tall grey woman conscious of lead

highest town in England — window
spangled with the flags of all diseases
some I never had never heard but didn't ask

strange country to be Sunday in
tell the gods by their colors
then he hid himself in what described him

name of a sickness shape of a boat
carried overland by silent travelers
how hard they struggle to come to water!

every molecule waiting to disperse
the intimate atomies of perfume
are you the truth or just smell like her?

52.
The dawn had less to say today
I stained it with one dream
answered deep cushioning cloud

light has the loudest voice of all
I keep feeling these birds are people I knew
they cluster the deck and want something from me

all that desire stuffed into one stone
I held the sky in my hand
wanted it for you, still won't let it go

watched the strange light with no sense of awe
what was my body not telling me
swift theology of seeing things,

waves tell me hearing is healing
quiet afternoon the ocean speaks
how to tell inside from outside

just for one moment the sea became solid
then flux came back, the UFO last night
winked out as I watched, distance never sleeps

in Wampanoag language means a piece of the sea
but maybe names mean nothing really
a name is just a cry in the dark

all the husbands round their wife
each claims her and she claims all
such power it is to be in the body

like a calla lily idling on a Berkeley fence
far from the rigors of Willard Quine
but white, almost luminously scentless

light up the mind leave the rest alone
I cried but she laughed with her haunches
and it was time at last for that boat to leave

will I remember this rock when I stumble
will the first religion of all claim me again
or will I cling to a low branch and see her

herself the last religion sitting on the stone
so far from me her mind can be at peace
but peace is too busy a word for that lucidity.

53.
Catch the river before it starts to flow back
you have a rock pool garden
the lesser celandine speaks to the liver

of course we live by color
what else is true
line is a Greek abstraction

or an Irish spell to make you love me
a line is an abyss in silence
a noisy gap inside the alphabet,

a cleft, rip, cloaca, fissure, wound
from which silence heals itself and you
the kind of silence the waves make coming in.

Are words like these just willed,
or wanted from afar?
clouds form the lips of a smile

why should I not believe
what speaks so clear? The moon
had little to do with this,

it was the sun, *die Sonne*, Lady *Grian*, who
in her modesty blazes up so bright
the cave inside me glimmers with strange alphabets,

Plato has little to do with this, this is love
mind yearning in matter
and the sea keeps egging me on.

54.
Things the gull remembers
when we were young people could be mean
always carry with you something red

where are all the mean people now
Apes in *Avernus* lilted from a song   *TC*
agathodaimon household serpent luck

old men at the window young men at the door
then it was morning, the light went out
I woke from a friendly family out of Jersey

how hard it was to write my name
simple as it is in numbers
they were patient and American

I wanted them to live with me
innocent and good, all because
I drove to the beach and never got there.

There, I have been faithful to my dream,
the bones of it, and god send I be
true to the dawning rainy day,

Kiche day when all those who have died this year
move from earth's penumbra
out into eternity 13-Death, who knows

who knows what happens to the dead?
We all know — but we don't remember
like the capital of Mali or the date of Waterloo

my past lives *slipped my mind* we say
sometimes a life ago's on the tip of my tongue
maybe enough to ken the times of day

rain comes to limber the ground
the earth stands up in us
there is no story.

55.
I thought I would miss you
but you're all there inside
avenue kept clear for some parade

old-fashioned blue policemen am I still alive
but you are inside me now
a smile more laughing than Brahms

why were we where we were or anywhere
there is no story and it does not say
write it on the back of an envelope, address the dead

they come to life, cormorants
spring out of the waves and fly—
I am not less than thee, O bird

(the year your mother died
a gull snatched a snake from her back yard
omens when you look, when you remember

female blackbird sudden in my house
fluttered around a sealed room disappeared
my mother died days later

such interventions in human order
give rise to something more than science—
forgive these stanzas, they hint at truth).

56.
Be patient with me it's raining
the wet flag flaps in the wind
nothing else says anything

a salesman or seducer's spiel is called a *line*
what does that say about poems
do we slip a doubting sweater on before we read?

Too long too long Gongula at the gate
let her in or you'll starve for sense
a German word that means 'to die'

the horizon is always halfway home
rearrange the tiles in this mosaic
no color lost but different loves display

how lucid water makes the air
wipes the streets clean of us
the girl just wanted to know everything.

57.
Rescue the unicorn from unbelief
as long as we think it, it stays in the world
all the lovely monsters lost that way

the important thing is to keep your name remembered
repeated out loud for a blessing
hero's name a cairn of stones in Thessaly.

58.
This island faint taste of stateless society
everybody does something, nobody makes them
unless the land itself compels

place makes us be as it needs us to be,
I am from island too always grounded by water
and the wind as mistress of us all —

no sound in a vacuum, no breath —
the ocean tells us, our thoughts
its dreams, our deeds its memories.

And by memory I mean measure
how the Shape of the Ædifice comes into View
and tells you that you are you

you meek young person on the Grand Tour
snuffling the cocaine of being different
you think, yet somehow you actually are,

no names, please, not yet
the fog has barely lifted after a life of rain
soon we'll see all the way to Portugal

by my reckoning just over the horizon
black sand with pale bodies sprawled
testing our vocabulary to descant on your lusts.

59.
This is that Elsewhere you always craved
full of clichés and champignons
don't worry you'll remember later,

just don't go there, ever,
your business is shod foot on cold earth,
look around you, your work is here

Nobody wins at this not a game
but everybody plays, next morning is prize enough
eating doughnuts in the back seat

bodies pressed together
physics is all about excuses
what the electron really wants

engine coughing in the fog
could you sit still and stop changing anything?
Be a three-cent stamp on an old envelope

no, don't bother to remember
so much your weary eyes have held
all the colors of the world

turned into towers and pyramids
you built a house a dozen times still stands
its shadow shields kind neighbors

you live by hope alone.
And then the ferry left,
kids leap from the dock

ceremony of freedom
we are fish in a basket
and no one knows the fisherman

weather-worn window watching the fog
the sun is on fire eight minutes away
already shadows are happening we live by signs.

60.
But was I listening
the cost of anything overheard
Scotch broom vanished fragrant from the hill

wind whacked the ice-bound aspens
winter felled many
the Other Life that vegetation lives

miracles we share and do not share
she sat beside me and explained
everything is your sister, see?

61.
No cloud sun on dew grass sheen
dawn stains away in the new heat
slight dawn of little after bird call — day

and who's the birthday girl
holding two ears of corn?
Who is America?

A dream is a riddle
no day can ever solve
that's why we sleep again

to meet her, the answer
a myth on pale legs
stretching out, a road through the sea

let all the stories tell at once
I dared to lecture her
she dared to let herself know how she is loved

only it wasn't love it was learning
grape arbor at midnight by the garage
and all the words a tender flight of stairs.

62.
I would be a green man covered all in leaves
burbling love at you in unknown tongues
you understand me all too well

languages of angels and of men
the Night Story keep mum by day —
dawn is where it's truest —

the trouble with a play, it's always in front of you
in front of everybody else
it's how we use the Greeks that troubles me

I want to think about the choices
a joyous animal selfishness innocence and fleet
free from all hegemony but love

would be a gentle way of saying it,
rescue Antigone from her false choices
we have no real choice but to be

be loud as we can be
love them all and say everything
and make the foolish harps of God resound.

63.
Lens of a mute lamp wakes in sunshine
wind flirting with the elm tree
I am not the only orphan in the world

the leaf has holes the rock has quartz
we live by discontinuity alone
that's why I breathe you in, crystal,

the force that makes a house fall down
also makes Apollinaire,
we are Krishna's cattle shambling to his flute

write your own words into my play
don't just sit there watching it, enter and renew —
tell the real story, tragedy too hot for most to bear

I admit I smell of ink
but the pen's gold nib gleams in the sun
and they agreed with me in dream with their hands.

And Gunnar spoke "I will not leave this island"
because his horse stumbled on the shore
language knows you where you are

crocus then lilac then rose
what else is time good for
Miriam, are you my sister with such pale arms?

64.
Homage to A.E.'s grand-daughter Pamela Haig
who lent me for months on end his painting
of *Briid* herself, goddess of wisdom,

a lovely woman standing on a hill.
She has blessed my life ever since
writing every day dream-gaelic in English.

Her painting rested on my books
and told me more than they could
thank you, Pam, your amber wisdom

Bright Briid the whole world is a fire
she holds the flame of in her cupped hands
 its flicker makes our tongues seem to talk.

65.
No one buys me anymore
I am copper
but Venus loves me as her own

he scribbled on a cloud
mistaking it for his napkin
slobbering a bit and the sun laughed

isn't that enough of a story
or how the Grail came back to Wales
or King David's gilt bronze harp

found buried under the zenana
wrapped snug in his wives' old clothes
by Solomon the King?

Or how the mackerel clouds above me now
form a mighty chalice
whose base rests above the Nashawena foreland

something I've never seen before
and who can say what wine is in it
or if water only, then what that water does

I want to drink it down, gulp, not sip
it would cure me of the silences inside
all my babble can't seem to spill

how water can be so flat and so deep-carved at once
perfectly still and always on the move
like sunlight balanced on a soaring gull

the things outside are only there
to make the inside stuff speak
and vice-versa, the angel said

when she caught me listening too hard
to what wasn't being said
angelic intercourse save one for me

forgive me for everyone I ever knew
until the peonies come out again
and I can whisper all their names

animal accurate to the rising sun
so she will love them too
and hold each one in her endless care.

66.
Caught in the image, a heart breaks free
angels come in cars, the light changes
careless (carless) counting adds up to one

I walked with you along a country road
but I was alone, the two of us together,
we didn't even look up to see if clouds.

Panorama is seeing all
means really looking around
talking is waking

rain is reign (*pouvoir* = *pleuvoir*)
words keep us in our place
Warning: Men Talking

every parliament, where the deep
tones of Big Ben boom out blah blah blah
and in their beds the nation trembles

power of the unexamined
the word that slips out
the word that drives the mind on rails

hearing is fearing
but hearing covers up our fears a little
but you can't hide the sky

that blue tycoon up there
 keeps reminding —
soon we'll be left alone

with clouds and other
memories (that's all they are), alone
with our anxiety or Debussy.

67.
In old-time shoe stores
clerks eased new shoes onto our heels
Try these on, they said

as if the shoe we snuggled in
were the same as destiny, the ready-made
fate that we let ourselves fit into

sun hot on my face, mother,
but all I see is cloud,
piece of ivory, stick of chalk

Cassandra smoothes her dress
along her hips along the way to destiny
she of all women knew what Death was hiding

unconcerned she walked
tired of the deadly quibbles of human men
who know so little, who have to kill to make sure

she stroked her thigh, Is this my fate?
toyed with her hair, Are all these strands
the scattered lines of all history?

Metrical epic of a lone woman
lived the crowded congress of all the voices inside her
o let me hurry to you, silence

yards away you hear the ferry engine throb
glad or gloom they flee the island
soon, I mourn the way we misheard her

but it rained on Waterloo and nothing happened
nothing ever changes only the look of things,
cars go no faster than horses but the clock is changed

Time is different now
never lets us see it naked
that animal in whose fur we parasite

I was so close to revealing a mighty secret
but the bee buzzed by, a nameless
dark thing skied across my sleeve

and a chickadee perched nearly:
do not tell, you're too close to being right,
only tell us what you do not know.

68.
It can all be explained
the coral reef the crime of passion
but who can live the explanation

choughs and sparrows in another nation
sailboats few but *far between* is where
I want to go on living

trapped in the human market,
giving comfort to my fellow hostages
the kings and commoners of earth

for we are here since birth
but death will not set us free
only a new beast philosophy

it sang till I woke
the way things speak
out of long thinking

years they lurk beside you
then suddenly declare
o please be there to answer them

by writing down the words they make you hear
then give them to one another
and call it *scop* or poetry

scope and shop and something *far between*
lyric of the water resting
song of heat ascending

why do we think that anything comes down?
It all is surging
through us and around us

the brief silence we call yesterday
finding my way to a difference
ice crystals in the June night

overturn the obvious
and there it is
the miracle again you always knew

cloud over rooftop
catbird sings in the bayberry
feta crumbled on tomato

the radiant particular
it's waiting for you
and then it will be there

here, in the only.
word turn Earth
taste what I have stored

I come to thee again
full of clock towers
animals with wings infest the air

up here they call a porch piazza
why are there soldiers in the square
dreams are animals that infest the day

lock the morning doors, my citizens,
this ink absorbs all stains
all sins are solved in fluency

violet as an afterthought
revision is a mainland thing
an island is spearhead quick

the quickest thing on earth is resting mind.
I trade you all my secrets
for the silence of your sleepy ears

start and stop like elderberry
something tumbles at the gate
who is this darkness really?

69.
Can't see the sky tonight
when will the moon come back
we sent her out to buy some cake

the kind lovers eat together.
You who claim to be my other,
what do you know of hunger in the dark?

Wake because the sparrow does
no choice but to begin
enjambment common in the actual world

rare bird in music —
kittiwake, folk etymology, a shore
with rounded hillocks, who goes there

open as a canoe, that wound on water,
lift the window shade to make the sun come up
language is the stepchild of repression

every word a Freudian slip?
But there are angels in it,
or they come from it and tell us truth.

Sooth we used to say
as if to know the real
was also to be comforted and soothed.

Rigorous dark, long march to morning!
Don't hide yourself from me,
I know you're in there, here, a member

of all that is remembered,
you stand before me
guilty of being my mind.

70.
I think the light is waiting to begin
or is that just me
muttering my dead language again,

Proto-Indo-Lollipop
I keep talking cause it tastes so good,
bear with me as I with my self,

you at least don't always have to be me.
Walk among aspens
tremulous quiet of their grove

here is a picture of me trying to fly home
shorter and fatter than these trees,
free me from my apparency

(first selfie 1839
man with wild hair and open collar
a face escaping from emulsion)

(or if that was some trick
I'm happy to be taken in,
every Trickster is a Noah

rescuing us from the deluge of the commonplace
by sweet prevarications and allurements,
come to my sweat lodge on the moon)

almost see the other island.
Language happens to us on its own
you don't really think all this is me —

I sinned against grammar
she woke me in the night
trailing her long pale hair across my eyelids

the trouble with death is you'll never sleep again —
living we are made free by our bivalve life
two-thirds here and one-third god knows where

somewhere dream can find us and make new.
Now I am a man in the lit window
writing glorious nothing in particular

the rigorous mathematics of a waking dream.
My hand in her pocket —
what more can science say?

71.

"Open all the rat holes" he cried   *HvH*
succumbing at last to the thinking world
all round him, no more matter

in the way of mind, all things sentient
and the sea on fire. His servants hurried to comply,
like men who had thought all this already long before.

Greet the day the way an old monk does
ceremonious Middle Kingdom way
dawn fresh glimpse of Paradise

because this only ever is,
seen through Buddha's blue eyes
we scandalously some of us wear too.

Is it demon in the blood or just Irish
nobody stops me when I walk down the street
stood in front of the house where I was born

"Where are you from, stranger" a neighbor asked
somewhere in me it still weeps for such estrangement
home has to be the other side of now.

72.
The plain grandeur of Whitman
solemn, immediate, not too smart
for its own good — that's the American key

to open the music room in this old house,
dust on Ginsberg's Hindu harmonium,
score open on piano where Duncan last tried Brahms.

73.
Secret thoughts of crocodiles
or what the white chalk cliffs
on Gayhead think as they crumble

hylozoic matter is alive *hylonoetic* matter thinks
things are sentient
a red truck passing downhill agrees with me.

Make it more so till it is.
This is my manifesto for the eternal theater,
make the same different, the different same,

spare hypocrites since we all are,
but punish kings we all would be,
from dismal stars set every woman free.

74.
Outside in the sun inside in the rain
all ye know on earth
I send you appetite to know something more

Give me a minute to excuse the rowdy light
clustering at the window
night could come again and spare the dream

or not know the words that come in me
language as *jouissance*
of course but I don't know what they mean

the words, come drop them on my skin
back of my hand so I can feel but not grasp
so I can learn by touch

the simplest things they mean,
a Christian battling the light
urgent reverie of the unawakened

fire on the desk
the sea stills thought
those women dreamt me in.

Stop. Before the sun
the sea is pure answering.
Later the French part comes

guessy wordwork of Blanchot and Nancy
dreamwork bruises of Derrida —
how young the heart is habit!

Keep singing as you were,
tender miracle a cotton thread
light squeezing through what I think I mean

what else is worth discussing
the six persimmons on no table   *Mu Qi*
the cost of milk?

Spread ink around the room
see if it sticks in shapes that look like words
read them out, you assassin of the alphabet

make signs no one can read
and make them so bright* everyone will understand
*a technical term meaning "overflowing with itself."

75.
In Fairyland they dream you on
the Queen's cut-thought henchwomen
summon you to mute observance

followed by your balbulous excitement—
what did you see?
Were you even looking?

Did you see us as we passed
stately dancing, reflection in a glass of water?
Here every son becomes your daughter,

caves inside words
animals on painted feet
nuzzle me awake

was it you after all?
Does all form partake of this geometry
this and no other, this weightless fruit?

But where is your hand when you are dreaming?
Writing rescripts for the Emperor, you slave, *écrivain*,
free as a brush stroke only for a moment is,

an eternity.
The word walked by and licked my ear,
forgive me all my well-meant absences,

my smile at those I dare not touch.
No photo ever showed me smiling.
Fact. The inner smile evaporates in light.

That's why my deepest worship is in night
when I be you what I really am
or think I do, good morning, love.

76.
Crimes of mercy, feeling sorry for oneself
the bars are full of me
and fishermen at early morning —

who feels sorry for the fish?
There are no permissions —
you take your risks,

your meadows and your maidens —
5000 years later we read from tablets again —
all that changes is what we oil our hair with

my lost Assyrian beard,
the wingèd bulls of Nineveh
who one day did carry me right here.

77.
If I can see it I must be me—
go back to sleep, the sun is finished with you,
she spoke your daily gospel portion

sleep now, go back to your cartoon.
Graveyard jokes, harps in the harem,
a place apart, walled round with thinking.

Sleep now and be my odalisque again,
let me stroke your hip reclining
and take that very line as measure,

measure and rule and follow it
and find out where a true line goes
over the hill and into the heart?

Let this be a little song between us
meaning not much but hanging around
back of the mind the way music does

a long time after you hear it.
That's your Sargent portrait I'm painting here,
as usual a century too soon.

Song, come out to sea.
The sun is alone with me.
I'm not as lonely as I glean

we sound like each other
the numbers set us free
one for her and all for me.

Tomorrow is the solstice
children running down the hall
carrying a cold candle to light from her touch.

78.
There are many parishes in Fairyland
and priests of many genders tend their flocks
joyous hence unruly citizens

 no rule but the moment
and the moment lasts forever.
I went in one of them, a chapel

twelve-sided and full of light, no altar
stood there but a Person all alone
in the center of the space collecting all the light

and everything I know comes from her mouth,
mixed, confused, annealed
by all the colors in the abstract windows

for in that country no one dares
to draw a picture, for every image shown
instantly comes to life and flies away

or walks or bites or loves you
according to its nature and your own.
So I reached home shadow intact.

But the one I saw there at the hub of light
I could discern no features of face or limb
just the out-welling charity that held me

and forgave already all my sins to come,
mine and everyone's, so huge
that small chapel suddenly became.

79.
In thrall to the thrust
the blood's concerto fights against the still.
Harmony happens — it can't just sit there

waiting. Dolphins in the channel, see?
They wonder what we're doing here
which is more than we do,

how feebly we are philosophers.
Someone not far off is broiling fish,
a poor being in its private hell

while folks stand by with brown bottles in their fists.
We demons.
The bright world is listening to me.

And the wind too has a shape
carving through the clouds,
Guardi's Venice sky over Vineyard

I have lost the proper name of everything.
Shape of a shape!
These hills hide ancient human ruins —

maybe all hills do.
Maybe we carved this planet out of thought,
afflicted molecules with purpose

then we rested, slept,
woke up and thought some other
made this while we were sleeping.

80.
I am tired of the muscles in my body
tired of how my legs feel on the ground
wake to a chorus of birds before the light began

longest day of the year and I had to be you
superintend the fashioning of light
light tastes different on an island

tick bites and long-neck clams and weather says you
my thought turns Mongolia and dusty and vast
the birds stop singing? is the whole thing a dream?

and if so, whose?
Little the light gains, can see the house across the road
big family sleeping in the dark

but where did that depletion come from
that sang me from the beaks of birds
muscles? legs? footsteps? wings?

Who are we when we speak?
I want to talk about oranges
and not have you think about the sun

With weird ideas about the gender of inanimates
left too many hostages in childhood
I am a smaller congregation now

thank you, dear Walter, island brother,   WW
voices fewer, deeper,
still trying to burrow through

the awful silences of human speech
where every word says Love me or I die
and take you with me

a word, a lone assassin,
a redeemer.
Open the bloody window

let the bloody light gush in,
this is my body too
he said and slept before the light could touch

this too is my body
I thought he meant, island,
sleeping woman, ocean, saying so.

81.
As if we were signaling to a star
far off, this earth full of spies,
slipshod agents of another heaven,

words wearing sunglasses, words wearing cleats
climbing mountains that are not there,
the dragons won, the maidens bound we wake again

don't you get tired of being right
notebook fallen from a cloud
this you're reading is a foreign language

out of fog the rain explains
everything knows us
no empty baggage load on board,

companionable shades, citizens of memory,
solemn tedium of other peoples' lives
o don't explain yourself in words

let me ponder the curve of your shoulder
you found a pleasant wooden bench beside the church
we sat in shade and looked at Gothic

as Stanford White imagined it this hot day
the memory now is soaked with rain
and I dreamt huge churches in Manhattan

smoke grey like old rubber
vaster than anything around, midtown
and even in the dream I knew they weren't there

but those were what I wanted,
a world of monuments and carved stone
bigger than anything should be

ceremonious, archaic. I slipped in
and found old people in a fancy restaurant
one of them called me Sonny, they all wore hats

another past I carved out for my mind
between your breath beside me
and a shock of wind kissed the wet glass.

82.
It's getting to it now
the thing I have to say
lost in language but alive in light

what can it be that asks so much of me,
Rilke with Rodin in Paris,
chestnut trees of Zurich blossom red and white,

getting to it but there is no it here
this is my 8th Symphony
music lets the words come clear

every word a gate
every sound a going in
translate the sound and know

this is where language wants to go
let it,
be outrageous in your obedience

raindrops on the windowpane
a battlefield of light
all the soldiers are on the same side

we are outpatients all
summer solstice
eternity means outside of time

we have the same heart
I am weary of my appetites
but not of what they desire

trivial glories of late morning
New England Sunday no church in sight
fine empty chapel with a fish on the roof

Fish-gods were good enough for our fathers
don't forsake the ocean that aimed us so well
already we have almost touched the sky

that orange too is on no table
sun coming out like sun coming out
I mean like a woman at a window

we love art because it never stops
doesn't know how to, its touch is permanent,
I walked by Leibniz's house unconscious

Freud's house, nobody home,
Melville's welcomed me
I sat at his table like a man eating an orange

there was no orange, book after book
it tasted like music,
left nothing behind but everything.

83.
I meant mahogany
but the wood was pine
I lit some shavings of it

and lo! the fire was the same
it has no dialects
and no one disobeys —

so many words I have
for only one answer
I think about you standing before me

and all the images recede
like books I've read or songs forgotten,
thingliness alone is present.

I'm trying to say *you*
to a thing, to every thing,
dust devil in Arizona I almost saw.

84.
She has stripped all her names away
and now is human, moving
to a music she can't hear

because hearing is made all of names
worship, church in the chest
the thing he thinks with, heart,

happenstance. The green of trees
reaches up the air. Mansard
roof aimed at heaven

so Protestant our little world
opera every minute
I raise my voice, something like a word

it comes to meet you
engine puffing, rails gleam in moonshine
surely it will take you home

this word will be there with you
capsize your smug kayak
plunge you in the meaning of itself

you castaway in a horoscope
you movie I liked but saw already
then suddenly you are new

never till now have I seen you as you are.
Indian paint-brush at the door, honest indigo
we were born to be together.

85.
The house has no door
you have to dream your way in.
Maybe nothing real ever has a door —

your self unselfed as you go in.
No one knows the weather in there
or who can whistle a cloud up for you

my father was Queen Victoria
that much the orange told me
Berlin doctor made me eat nothing else

so I decided to stay awake a week
just business days, the weekend was for God
always closer when you sleep

I was in America and why not
an ancient statue buried under East New York
came to its surface and told me what I needed

learn Greek, honor women, take long walks.
It could have been Kant I was reading,
the statue's eyes were just as much of stone

86.
Unfamiliar bird
dark against the rising sun
is saying something

what? to whom? do I dare to interpret?
a world full of messages
from no one to no one

I follow my footsteps
to a place I've never been,
tell Dr. K. about it, hypnotize me

so I think I'm wide-awake
full of brambles maybe and thorny
raspberry bushes dense flowering white

me or the place
who can tell us apart,
things fall together

that's the real trouble
Jean-Luc, if sex and art
are so much alike in their pleasing

bad news for art
since sex is art enough for most of them
so let's keep that likeness secret

keep all likeness under wraps
occult philosophy, be silent
read the signature of things

or hyphenate all things' names
the way they do in Spain
or double-barreled hipster children

JLN

sun-grass fall-stone window-moon
language lets us
only the mind breaks off

mortal mind she called it   *MBE*
as opposed to mind
slow down and think in words ahead.

You met me long ago in Prague
drank weak tea in Paris
before any of your famous wars—

to live in language is to live forever
why do you say that?
because I do, or it does,

are you asking me to prescind?
I don't know the meaning of that word
or any other when the cows come home

all I meant is I have lived
longer than you could listen
and death is the furthest thing from mind.

87.
Build the sound into the sky
follow it as it finds its way home
know the house — bird perch on roof

this is the only place
it must be, a window looking out to sea
or caveman's cave the human mouth

words rush out and capture you.
Odysseus snows
cantilevered structure of attention

and when that bridge falls down
we raft away on wreckage
as if all going were a little country stream

we stood by once remember
who were we then
rising sun in cloudless sky

sometimes sounds inside the body
a message from some self of me
I don't have diplomatic relations with

so don't go down the cellar stairs
to find the mysteries of our own house
and that's how it should be

we are hollow inside, spacious with delight,
mind coursing over an endless ocean
placid as a dictionary

half-eaten orange on the table,
a woman would put a plate beneath it
but this sleeping man leaves it on bare wood

I dreamt there was no dreaming
and everything was real
that was the strangest dream of all.

38.
Burrow in the light
see where it leads you,
where does light leave you,

my father teased me. I used to say
Where does the road leave?
I must have known already

roads have minds of their own
roads carry us
If we could stop all striving

we would be suddenly there
road's end, where the road leaves us
and we are where it knows we need to be

but how not to strive?
Wu wei, they suggested, *Do nothing.*
But nothing is the hardest thing to do.

89.

(Tale of the White Stone)

I am the morning sun
she said, come follow me,
I am all going and no doing

and every being lives from my quietude
(the things you hear when you look out at the sea)
so much to hear and nothing there—

it's the story not the story's end that charms us
we love the ongoing, it lives us for us
crisis is continuous

and if it should be only this, at least this is.
You taught me language cries Caliban
fierce at not having been left to learn it by himself

mistakes from which new sciences arise
new texts, new moons in sad old skies
or the glorious fifth-night moon over Avalon.

And then she brought me the white stone
it had been everywhere she said
it rose to you on the sea, so small.

"No priest but the perfected" you,   *MBE*
she said, but were they waking
when it spoke?

Listen to the white stone:
I have been the whole sea
now listen to me: things wake up

you can play all the roles yourself
lose your hat to the wind
your shoes to the mire

truly, the gods love relativity
they bless all the answers to no question
leave some barley at the cave mouth and go home

there is only weather, understand?
The dream was terrible with animal —
they don't end clean or quick

"we live in the flicker"   J   JCK
seal of the confessional
I have told you enough

now solve me into radicals
the kind a scholar inks on his fan
to keep the air talking in his solitude

what am I made of? I asked
not much, he answered, just enough
sometimes, petals of a wild rose fallen

so many roses and the surf high
a set of careful variations on no theme
nothing complex, just other people.

Last sneer of darkness before dawn
live a long time in
dream awake all that stone collected

to be so small and white and far away
and here in my hand she gave it
when cloud came over the cold sea

Listen to me I'm not talking
that's why listening is so important
a different street each time you raise the shade

twinkling lights of nowhere
as if to see at all is to be inside a house
live there believing all the evidence

pick a scrap of paper up and that's your bible
doesn't matter who wrote it
finished words wash away all authorship

"as if I knew the way there
a gull does, goes,
guided fatefully by appetite alone"

it said, last line definite,
faith is fate, you believe in what happens
so it does and goes on happening

you're caught in it
like a gull trapped in the sky
just be, beautiful in your constraints.

Why do we say have sex not do sex
because we like to possess things
even things that aren't ours to touch —

the trees don't walk,
they swallow time
and use it for their rituals,

leaves, colors, fruit, sheer permanence
you read the years in their fallen wood
while you were busy wandering around.

Hold the stone to your forehead what do you feel
someone opens a gate and the sea comes in?
live alone in a lighthouse?

but what do you hear?
the rigors of a violin
polemos, king of all music,

never marry a performer
all they can do is manipulate—
an audience so why not you?

Enough sagesse, old priest,
morning yearns to suffer
to silence the dream in work and worry,

don't be so smart with people's lives,
ignorance also teaches us,
I blame myself when no one else around

a human is *something else compressed* —
hence the many in me, the many more in you—
to be in love is like immigration,

becoming a citizen of a population
languages you barely hear
just stay here long enough you'll understand

how I love the stone you gave me
albestone, marble from the moon
before it left earth, can think of only this.

Having nothing more to offer saying so
I stayed home yesterday and watched the kids
scramble through the dictionary

but the dream caught me anyway
small tiger under the aspidistra
fear tormented me

I ran through the house till there were only flowers.
How do they find me in the night
their eyes are closed their teeth are sharp

it was landscape sucked you in
you had no protection from those hills
as if you wanted to come home

and all you recognized was green.
They tried to catch me too but I drove fast —
yet then I slept, and woke inside them

we belong in there, blossoming indigo in green.
Yearning for nameless things too safe
we *specify*, and perish from denial if we do

that's why the hills matter
— o you can see them north of Margaretville —
they teach inside that nothing matters

we build things we forget
others find and use
loss by loss we run to mind

bright openness inside the smallest room
the promised gleaming emptiness, *śunyata,*
semina, the seeds of all.

And then I stroked my fingers up the wall
to make it part of what I meant
it answered me by opening a door

so dark I went in step by step
then a thought came and I stopped counting
and stood there domiciled in thought

but thought means nothing till you write it down,
allēlois, to one another
where they play in the hot sun

morning, and no one bothering to hear.
That's not despair, that's liberty,
a hummingbird choosing, choosing, being gone.

Land heats fast, warm air rises,
cool air comes in from the water
to take its place — sea breeze

it is supple as an argument
and movement never stops
and love of course operates just so

hot goes to heaven cold wants to get warm
it's just physics, don't make a fuss—
but physics makes the biggest fuss of all.

90.
Frivolous mind on solemn goat
mounted — bronze. Honest to everyone
except himself — silver plate. Childless.

Staring out the window at the rain — gold.
"It was not raining." — carved peach pit.   *SB*
His lost love — ad-face poster on a bus

London. End of story. Now
the miracle begins. Slept nine hours.
Opened the door. It's all right, the air said,

It's all right. The catalogue
has begun. Sell or buy, what difference.
You are only your material, plus a little silence.

91.
To believe in karma believes in science
science is the liturgy of causality
(yes, but when can I stop being me?)

the lost mine, god on a goat,
hammer round the neck,
girl riding a swan

all our armies march away from Troy
(cold coast in Karelia, where epic began)
every war ends in defeat for both sides

shut up, she said, the only gold I ever gave you
is silence, as your father said
who hoarded it with green-eyed decency

when all I loved was excess
not *mēden agan* but again, again,
never let the story pause (there is only one)

oh you say these tricky things
rhombuses in round holes squeeze
to make me think you say but all I do is think

or more precisely I am you thinking.
Oh. Ohime! Opera all over,
more, more, *amore, amore, morte, morte*

an old man grieving by an empty bag.
Dialogue never ends, there's nobody here,
words lie in wait like tongues of the trees.

I could go no further on that road
the Roman troops well-meaning blocked my way
who wants to go to Spain anyhow they cried

ma in Ispagna the long line of lovers reaches the coast
Atlantic where the Grail poured out
and made the holy ocean holy

like a burning branch to the fire drawn
to concentrate the essence of the god-man
by dispersing it through all the world

by water only, first language of all,
there is a name for such theology
and a sneer for every saint,

am I real enough to guess
the final cause of going on,
locked churches, midnight diners,

friends you never need to see again,
that pelican at rest on the red sand,
gull caught in the sun's last rays?

92.
Sit down I want to tell you about yourself,
how do you spell Florida, sit at my table,
I know so much about you you don't know

Kids at the next booth were laughing
but not even at us, we survived
in a cloud of innuendo, a communion,

the sharp strong wine of just listening.
Listen. I know your future if you assent,
but one must assent to what one is

before one can become oneself. Yourself.
I can see in your eyes the art work
you will make, soon, soon, and be attended

by all the wordy muses of the galleries
and you will be as they say happy.
No don't go yet, the prophecy continues

only if you consent to being you—
I can't do it for you, consent, assent.
By then the coffee's cool enough to drink

now no words need come between us.
But words are what we are,
noise in each other's mouths.

Isn't time to end these sly encounters
unkowns talking in the dark
ignotum per ignotius explain?

All these people are just things as they are.
is there a difference between hand and machine?
Birdfeeder hanging from the sky

that's why, the alchemists who run the earth
this experiment in mind's matter
have to keep the temperature just right

in this alembic earth. The world
is made of time and of forgetting.
Heatwave in Karachi, hundreds dead,

peccator, piscator, is fishing the first sin,
take from the ocean and give nothing back,
soft cold down there to heat our meat?

A way of passing time only males could choose
house full of men, agony of space,
11 miles to Gayhead on an easy sea.

93.
Because we have to begin again
loosestrife on no meadow here
sit in the cellar and bless the rain

pink patent leather heart and speaking Viennese,
the diner never closes, close the book,
it's time for blood normal to disperse.

Dispel. The alchemists sleep by their oven,
a small ancient vessel cracks in unwatched heat,
the unripe human spirit leaks out

becomes all of us — we need to be *finished*.
Looking at us from your usual distant star
the first thing you notice is we're incomplete.

That means we still need time.
That's why Time is still in the world,
an idiothermal chemical of theirs

to finish the job. Then we will be.
And there will be no more Time
and no need of Moon to measure it.

He spoke, but my eyes were on the girl beside him
older by millennia than he,
trembling with puberty and truth.

94.
There is no natural silence
that too we have to make
and so I have been working

thousands of years since I was
like Rosalind an *Irish rat*
and learned to gnaw,

and silence only lets itself be made
by bringing like-unlike things together close
so silence is the space that trembles in between.

Hence using language, whose words
are the cheapest materials of art
and we are poor, poor people in between.

Delicate assertions, bird lands on your arm.
Chickadee. Divot. Digit.
We count by fingers still

that's why there are so many of us,
20 million in Karachi so we can count the stars
or other weird projections of the local mind.

A man looking at the sea
this is a permanent thing.
It never goes away, the sea. The seeing.

A gull comes by like the Holy Ghost
escaped from a church window,
flies above our roof, *Gott mit uns* we cry,

and on the Baltic coast Cassandra sighs,
God is too much with us maybe she means,
all we have to give is being known.

We go from house to house explaining
until nobody understands.
Then, then we are free.

95.
Body and soul, plum, pelvis,
Eden, spoken command, written law,
string quartet = Woman, Water, Matter, Man,

Revelation has only just begun,
there are traces of the future buried in the flesh —
look in your hands and remember.   *SJ*

All I need is to begin again,
the weather and the ferry,
the dog who recognizes —

so many specifics and no rule,
no General Theory of the livelong day.
What bird is that? we're always saying

or Why does the red pale
when the light increases? *Phōs augei*
we used to say when we believed

Christ came for more than family values.
But the handle fell off the door
we can't find the inner chamber anymore

the "kingdom of heaven is within" meant meditate
you slackers, don't hide in church
from the bright secret in your heart

commit to memory is commit to madhouse
lost in there, democracy of the incoherent
day without a night

the Muses have fled in their canoe —
that's what he meant,
that word in a bottle, that spring?

Ile leape up to my God, the word is generous   CM
Faust still is leaping, rising like heat
from the fires of hell, must rise,

must find the skies, no one
can pull heat down, him down,
his ardor Edens him at last

another part of the island
over the moors and find the inmost pond
where two swans—

have I told you enough
or is it morning already
and I've kept you from dreaming?

96.
I am the only animal
I insist
let me look at water to begin

if I had the right
to open your hand
how much I'd have you do with it

but the steamboat full of musics
carried her out of mindshot
and only the river knew how to sleep

no river here thank God
I love them but I adore their mother
all round me

he wrote almost in shame almost the Truth
as near as he could bring his skiff
to that most dangerous shore.

97.
Bunny on the lawn. That's closer.
Almost truer. *Celer sicut cuniculus*
schoolboy Latin, o Memory you are such a slut

you come home with anything.
To see the ocean is completion,
that's what he meant to say. See.

He keeps losing the difference.
Penetralia. Open mouth.
Open the temple. Allegiance.

Northernmost point on the sun's path —
we see her moving, don't interpret yet
let her tell the long truth of being here —

the elm tree in front of this house.
And here she is, all of her names
splayed out in one syllable of light

(of course the sun is woman
who else gives warmth and light,
lucid intelligence?

Isn't it clear when Ahab says
I turn my body from the sun he turns
his back on all that women mean,

he, the solo crazy, phallo-focused to insanity.
The goal, the goal! And a goal
is always a revenge)

I wanted you to know all that
in case I forgot to make it clear,
sunrise on the calm Atlantic home at last.

This is the water where I was born
on a rock part of the rock I stand on
where far is near and everywhere is here.

So long it took me to discover
water is not matter
it is a kind of person who reasons us.

Writing is a submarine
gliding secretly below anything I mean
and every word gladly parenthetical,

everything we say is footnote to the unspoken.
To work on this one word
would be enough.

Analyze. Emphasize. Be pure —
the word will come
and you will welcome it aloud.

Here ends the lesson. *Übung* my father
used to say, *macht den Meister*, keep
doing it till it knows how in you

then you're a master. We grow up
—Leiris shows this — almost by words alone.
Or our deeds are *their* resonance out there

where people are, for whose sake
words came into the world
to guide, beguile and comfort them.

What we hear turns into our bodies
and what they do.
Otherwise it's just ink drying in the sun.

130

98.
Every day is Sunday morning here.
Trees see to that with their vestments
light and shade, wind with its liturgy

all quiet till the people come.
The us-animals, disturbers of the peace,
and with incurable nervousness

we jabber when other beasts would run away.
Or play machines to talk for us
so we can find (pray let me find)

the silences inside.
Smells like a tiger, moves like a stone.
Prays to itself the way water does

When you see it moving in a basin,
gently, no need to frighten yourself. Be water.
Flow everywhere, everywhere at home.

99.
Unfit for reproduction
like a murky varnish-darkened oil
or my children would be monsters

more selfish even than I
he claimed, but he was bitter
hearing *les voix d'enfants*

in the street, the lawns, the trees
the sacred silliness of their prancing around
intolerable innocence.

I shivered, retreated from his attitude, yet
I want a billion children
but not to own them. Let them be.

100.
Being inside a pearl
it seemed, the sky two hours back
washed the sea clean, and both took delight

then color came back
deciding against us the Mandarin
spoke a terse poem in Manchurian

and we were doomed to exile and blue mountains,
horizon a bow and we its arrow
and so I came to the famous two-way river

wanting everything, terrified of getting it,
my mind the shape of a caved-in barn
cows outside looking back in doubt.

What the bird sees when it flies away
a world so close to ours but not,
so I fly with him when I can

like Cocteau with Roland Garros
watching what does not have to be imagined,
the other ordinary out there.

So my vocation is vacation, analyzing emptiness
and my rich, slow, dull music comes from that,
and there too I see the shadow of her passing.

101.
As if waiting there all along
they were speaking when I woke
no easy language to my grief

Troll or Truscan, something lost
between the skin and the atmosphere,
garnet tossed from a passing Volvo

nothing but enigmas everywhere
and the hydrangeas haven't yet turned blue.
No wonder I need you so.

Read too much Shakespeare but not enough,
the Living Theater went away
we have to find language in living bodies

bring back my Babel to me
all the way from Arkansas or Bogart Street
there has to be Language driving the car

otherwise the body never gets there
and we leave darker than we came in
and language has to bring us home.

102.
Forgive dull interludes of social meaning
I live here too, a man goes fishing
it's all about kids and original sin

the basic text is living in the air
I hold the cellphone to my heart
it learns to beat from what it hears

just listen to you
living breath ill-dressed in speech
I see you through the gaps

all things show through
imagined bodies with real skin
all I meant to do was still

the noise of data rolling in
but got you instead
a hum like home.

103.
Dear Sophia — I just want
or need to get exactly
right what you told me:

mermaids don't live in the sea
they *are* the sea
and the pictures you see of them

are what the sea makes men think,
right?   because the sea
is not matter and not human, the sea is a person,

or more accurately water is a person
water is someone so many wheres at home.
Tell me if I got this wrong. Love Robert.

104.
I live here why can't I speak
the language better than a native flower?
because it knows its seasons and I don't

always in rut and never wide-awake
dreams mumble through my mouth
and people look at me

maybe that's all language does
says Look at me
like Bruckner's *Da bin i'* pounding at the doors

and they look at me sometimes with love
as if I were one more thought they had
last night before they fell asleep

(as I was going into sleep I met this man
his lips moved but no sound came forth
I touched him expecting to feel glass

but he was not me, he was another,
I read his lips, No room in this dream
and who is that stepping close behind?)

On a chilly morning interview the fireplace
warm afternoon, lagoon. Crow on long white sand.
Never wake up.

105.
Learn Icelandic. *I will not leave this island.*
The sky bigger today than ever
speak the idiom of cloud.

Prophecy is *speaking for* —
for whom dare I speak?
I thought it was you

beloved citizens, you whose thoughts
gelled in my heart too
and I spoke your desires —

is that not true, comrades?
you in your dirndl skirts fifty years ago
your hipster hats last year,

aren't you my lovers, brothers, selves,
selvedge of my being, where it ends
and you begin, don't you love clouds too?

If you love a cloudy sky you must love me.
He wrote, and the gull carried his words
to the clouds where the Sun was doing her washing

and she smiled at him!
Or maybe at the gull — birds
are not just naked messengers.

106.
Go in and see what the water says
beyond all the glad reflections
what is she saying down inside?

Or are we engineered to know
only surfaces since we ourselves are hollow,
filled exclusively with light

as she is filled with some mysterious ipseity
it is no business of mine to disclose
even if I knew such translucency.

107.
The ever arriving chariot
white one black one horse horse
it leaves it comes back

every time it happens my head holds more —
rain in a thunderhead waiting to speak
Lord, let it say what I mean

the only science is epistemology,
all the rest are just counting things
measuring forces and disappearances

only sometimes there are too many of a thing
then the other horses come
loosed from their chariot, their deed,

they come with war and plague
shadow of a big rock Arizona
speak softly while the snakes are sleeping.

108.
Wrong skin
by color alone
I have no voice to speak that wrong

no authority to know the hurt
that still goes on
all our years in this huge town

make fences higher than ever
money sets us at our neighbor's throat
incurable alterity of the stranger

and color colors everything
as if it were natural,
some basic evil like gender or disdain

our shame
my shame in my own wordlessness
let the words weep for me

it would not let me sleep
I rose to meet it
with my rusty sword

dream dragons have no fear of steel
for they are made of fear
and we fall down from feeling them

we have no instrument
talk funny and go to sleep
may the Lady bless you with oblivion

that final outpost of astronomy.
The enemy is always right —
that's where it starts,

this wisdom thing you hear about
wings on her hips and bells for her clothes
she is always with you if you listen

she taught me how the sea is made
how eels come home
and atmosphere an accident of ocean

drought comes from cruelty
anger dries the desert up,
I'm guilty of hydrolatry

we live by drowning
in what it does as air
and waves come round to waken us

But I am afraid of the dream
I mean the little one when we think we're sleeping
not the big one when we dream ourselves awake,

I don't even have tears
to blur the scene a little
or tell you that I'm sad

a face expressionless and mute
no doubt the rigid mask of root anxiety
fear so deep it feels like family.

109.
As if word could open after all
and we thieves creep in
where the velvet stalagmites whisper

in no wind but our own breath
insinuations of what we could not know
and we speak.

For as Nicholas points out   *NC*
(born by the same town as Marx)
how can we worship what we know?

How can we even know what we know?
only the unknown is worth our speech,
that chattering liturgy that says our prayers.

The person so vivid you saw in dream
you never knew elsewhere —
no wonder we fall on sleep

like a Roman on his sword
to flee the long defeat of day
hoping to see her face again,

his face, the boy, the bearded, the girl,
the Dream Ones come to you in motley,
appearances are pure snare

you think, but then they come again
and touch you in that sleepy place
and suddenly you're home.

110.
The storm talks.
It awes with energy
the seeming purposelessness of its wild,

enigma of the ordinary
immensely magnified,
why are things what they do?

Is there even anybody home?
And it doesn't need
me to tell you this—

I'm just some other thing
a noisy opacity
in its great howl.

I'm still here I think
trying not to make sense,
let it make sense and let me watch

deck furniture hurled all about
as if reproach: how dare ye
colonize Outdoors?

isn't it bad enough
you stick up houses to crouch in
then strew your stupid chairs out here

where everything else belongs?
keep your "indoor philosophy"   *JM to RWE*
locked in there with you,

cunning rats that you are
in the maze you make of everything.
The wind said. But the rain washed us away.

111.
The Trinity old Irish invocation
prodrome to any future prayer
this is a prayer

to the three great ones
but who are they
and where do they live in us?

we know they are three
we give them names
like people in a family, what else do we know,

Father, Child, Mother or Wisdom—
if its too frightening to think of woman
you call her a ghost

but you mean well
you mean the breath of light
red love pouring into the system

indigo calm in which you
like the greatest wizard in the world
get to read your own mind,

a miracle to know and be known.
In the name of the trinity
of so many names

let the prayer or reckoning begin.
Almost home,
the fish all safe in the sea.

112.
Just listen to where it goes and go there too
your part is always willing to begin—
air inhaled turns into light

outside and inside are the same now
when we breathe out again,
air's the way light floods into our heart

city is a prayer spreads out on all sides
light wipes cruelty from the heart
all the dualistic crap of you and me

because there is only you
and what I guess as me
is the smallest measurable part of you.

113.
Leave the invocation till the end
when the gods can decode
what manner scheming you invite them to bless

they don't want just anything I think
even wise words may not pass
saying wisdom is not the same as being it

as well they know
such a hard job it was even for a god
to get rid of everything but wisdom alone.

Try to believe me so I can trust myself.
we are mirrors to one another,
glass ashy or oily

but the outline true.
to see so many trees
after so much sea,

the worlds we choose.
Have I told you yet
all the things I mean? Yes and no.

114.
Vision is Eden again
the book tried to tell us
but priests turned it inside out

leaving the trees
was leaving Paradise
the apple just food for the journey

we didn't have to travel
but here we are a million years later
and she thought he was the gardener

but he was the man who broke down the door
so we could move in and out, in and out,
the space of spirit that works like home

where we come to be what we mean
since meaning counts
how many leaves we leave on the tree

and name them to cover us all over
we nude forgetters
we should live on light alone!

or are we only punctuation
in a never-finished text?
Or back in the meadow of the alchemists

where merchant booths offer silk,
wool to tempt us into language
since naked men can't speak

so all right linen me fur me
I will endure the sacrifice of speech,
the caution of being.

That's what it means to wake up,
eat breakfast in the Middle Ages
until we're in the Iron Age again

relentlessly into the past
to find that treacherous landmass
shifting and sneaking north

when first men had to buy their apples
with money stolen from the ground itself—
didn't they fear the *sa-bdags* who hid the gold

and hide it still, landlords of our earth
and always will, it is their house
we walk through thinking it my own?

115.
Curl it tense as a leaf
you found folded in on itself
snug in grey morning

an idea not yet ready to think
itself into your thinking—
wait for it, be a dog at your own doorway,

everything simple as in and out—
you don't need Dante to tell you that
durante, the man who lasts,

laughs in hell and weeps in Paradise.
Endure like him,
a sweet vagrant through the images,

buy a paper of pins from a peddler,
Roma maybe,
certainly Amor.

116.
Language as such
a tragic liberty
I am silent where it counts.

All I want is to give you yourself
but have only language to give it with—
such pride and such humility, a mess,

but whatever I may say
it's all about you.
And the sun comes around the corner

and makes the old rail fence glow—
fence is town is *polis* is definition.
See, we do live by light.

Christ I want to name every wave
mingle with the remotest
be a great-grandson of every flower

make up a new language
so I can fail to learn it and have to start another,
I want to be another for a while

so I can see if there's anything here
where what I think of as me
chooses (is condemned to) stand.

117.
Even here the storm's still talking
it doesn't know how to stop
only we do

we cherish our obstinate alone
our abstention from language
dare to call it 'silence'

but our *tais-toi* and stupid *schweigen*
is the enemy of silence, it's mute aggression,
resistance, suicide pact, act of war.

Real silence shares with everything,
only these birds shouting at dawn know it
only the thunder speaks silence best.

It is gospel hour, minstrelsy,
talking in tongues — doesn't matter
if you know what you're talking about

just keep talking,
the truth will out,
the inside silence will light up

meaning will happen,
fresh as these birds flying by,
dawn cardinal wanting at your window,

just to be particular, don't mind,
soft grey sky behind the trees.
There are still people I need to speak,

did you think I'd run out of stories?
Think again. Budapest, snakeskin, avalanche,
one woman alone in the whole city

holds fire cupped in her hands,
speaks Irish, sleeps in Paris,
walks barefoot through river-bottom mud

lives in a cathedral.
What else do you need to know?
She is your mother too.

118.
A novel is no way to tell a story
a novel is a way of rinsing time with language
a story is a bone

broken bones you find in the grasslands
your lustrous mind is rife with meat
mute circumstance to flesh out the bones

and set them walking all days on
in the same mind
where every story comes to live.

Match the bones with their shadows,
match silences to their sounds
and here your story is.

119.
Too much and not enough!
Truest motto of great art,
listen to her raving and rave too

to shape the flesh that lives for love
(the rocky road to Dublin)
(ruined chapel street lights few)

(change the words to turn the music on)
(*mood the more as our might littles*)
(fight on with gold-frame harp, cords of sinew)

(make a sound-box of your hollow cheeks
and rub your stubble — play a scale)
what I needed to say was another language,

words are the evidence of our neuroses
every word a Freudian slip
Analyze me in your lap?

Someone must be listening,
you can see the colors now
they all are green.

Listen hard to make the light come back
I'm not the captain of this ship,
a stowaway priest fleeing the inquisitors

and they are anywhere you stop listening.
The trees are the sea more than ever,
sky as bare as if I made all this up

when I'm just a piece of its puzzle,
an ambassador from amnesia,
but they endure my appetite for guesses

when a dictionary is pure lunacy.
Some of them don't turn away.
That's when the real silence breaks.

120.
Stare at the medicine till it starts to work,
let your taking meet its sending
and listen to the pain disperse

it's all in the thing thinking
your thinking learns to hear—
there is no lonely to a listen ear.

Only what I need
needs doing
the rest takes care of itself

the way I take care of the moon
the goat grazing on it,
all the sheep gone from the hill.

121.
Watch the future right in front of you
close your eyes you'll see tomorrow.
Under bridges shelter from going.

I like the hips of the day best
the edges where it's widest
the gloaming he called it   *SJK*

learned it from his mother   *FMK*
a hundred years ago
when they had more mornings and more evenings

can a man know more than his father
throw away the bible
the first rose has happened to the bush.

122.
Opal morning Talmud
we just need to stand under
anything for the first time again to get it,

she recruited me for her ocean
and then there were two swans
who had they been before?

Venus and Jupiter close above your roof
sole lights in this poor sky.
Cancel all the pronouns

there are just stars
witchcraft whenever people think
17 bullets killed him "in possession of a rock"

they will wake in the night and see his terror face
so hide your white stone in your pocket
hide your red stone under the armpit skin

hide your blue stone in the Franklin stove
let no one ever see your stones
or the stone will stop talking

and when the stones are silent
who will your mother be?
And what will your father finally say?

123.
Choose the rapt color
agencies of otherwhere
this pale pink flower

is a kind of knower
we may never get there —
peacock feathers.

What believers call God's Will
is Themselves in Control —
power to unmake whatever is.

The Queen of Silence
keeps coming up,
suit lost from the deck of cards

silence, whose symbol is a bell
without a clapper, a full cup of water,
a child asleep at the tide line —

at first I thought it was a seal
the way she looked up at me
from so far away.

124.
Sibelius violin concerto
ants on a pile of sugar
—do all ants share a common soul

or does each every ant have its own —
riddle me that, Cardinal Nicholas,
or tell me who I am

when I look up and say "I don't know"
the answer to some random question,
what is the capital of Burkina Faso

or what did Frobenius really mean?
Who is it who doesn't know?
does he have a right to use my name?

O darling clean your whistle
before the wind blows
or how will you know which is me

and which is the torpor of the idle isles
skimming its geography across the air
shaped like music but then you wake up?

I can't help language being there,
all I can do is use it up —
stare at the sea till your thirst abates.

125.
Smell the linden trees in flower—
STC's "lime-tree bower" but my prison
much smaller than his, inside my one body

and nowhere to go and still be me —
a childish problem like all the real ones,
whose road is it, and leaves you where?

However long it is it's just one fugue,
Lady Fox and Master Wolf
folklore leaves footprints in the heart

beast-scat we mistake for thought,
fox cub on your green table
only the random can help you now.

126.
compose by sentences
Lachenmann on Blennerhasset's island
rule the world by noise alone!

Woodpecker at the soffit!
Paving machine hovering outside,
lawn mower threnody,

don't trust the evidence
pretend to analyze the motivations,
lie on the couch of the sound and lie,

just lie.
By your deception we shall know you
and by our fibs be known.

127.
All-seeing eye
is where it starts
earthly terror

to be seen is to be known
to be known is to be wrong
(the visible world's a leaf

of what tree? Fig leaf
to hide my sex in?)
or be another and be free.

By sex the book meant agency
to be responsible
for everything that happens

Emily in uniform, armed against chance   *EPr*
we have no name but what we're called
'God' means what or whom we call

the reverent animal of us
quietly believing and knowing nothing
not because there is nothing to be known

but there is no we to know it,
chaste as human skin
maladies of touch

are you awake yet again?
Stay snug in these words I gave you,
faculty of speech children snoring in the night

sleep now,
the world won't last if you wake up,
you know you're sleeping when the eye stays shut.

Who knows who lives in the sky?
Gagarin had a look around and nothing saw,
didn't realize Nothing was there and could be seen

exactly, to shout down the hollow,
to answer the rain with all your skin,
yes! Of course there's nothing there —

it's all here, gold bright in the heart,
half-silence and half-echo
of the words that no one spoke.

128.
They're not pretty but they're young
they laugh and smile
they are the earthquake

they are vegetable as they can be
they grow things and think them at me
they wear weather and fear the moon

they comfort me with happy prattle
they forget me soon as I leave
they give me freedom like a stalk of celery

they explain animals to one another
they let me taste the ocean but not drown
they have hands that are always full

no wonder I am afraid
no wonder I can't remember my name
they fill the shopping bag and I am gone.

129.
It doesn't have a design
it has a rhyme you can't hear
Duncan taught us that

the structure of a disappearance—
a man willing to say anything
teaches everything

new kind of weather for new kind of mind
binary! dualist! give me a world
where no means yes and yes means I'm sorry,

the hummingbird teaches me code
coming and going is the only way of staying
here is the center of the world

Byzantium rises again,
post-Abrahamic, luminous and blue.
Am I the last pagan or the first?

what minds we'll have in a hundred years
all there waiting for you
and you are their only answer

isn't that what witchcraft is,
your skin slick with Oil of Listening,
the cold moon cracked open

to yield the midnight sun?
Hold it in your quiet hand —
action at a distance

someone singing in the field,
is it wheat or barley, night?
Where shall I say my Mass?

130.
Oaken parameters
by which I mean propose
a table beneath the sea

be there with me,
drench me a suppose
slipped into a certainty

wouldn't the moon be brighter then,
the bluebird land on a rock every day
content to behold you?

deep inside the inside
where the mother-game plays out
sleeping queens map out new domains

young surveyors swarming the boudoir
for this is natural
and nature is the only enemy,

it makes us do what we would not
and kills us in the end —
wherefore I have taken ship and vanished

into the holy druid mists of mind
where no "natural thing" can find me   *WBY*
and there I wait for every you

and that's the table set
shulchan aruch beneath the sea
followed your pale limbs to find the place.

131.
Consider the map.
Lines of the face,
some structural, some adventitious —

from age or other injury.
The colors in between the lines
are countries or shires or dialects,

you'll know when you get there.
Till then resort to folk songs,
pemmican, tales of Rim Ram Ruf   GC

because letters save us from the real.
Who's us? Read and find out.
The real is almost bad as nature is

choose the right verse and anything is legal
those who read the Bible understand it least,
leave it on the shelf and do as you please

just be sure to hurt no one, he said.
And here the green time comes again,
an afternoon is made for trouble,

If you had a life at all
you wouldn't need to die.
Logic is more terrible than Hell.

132.
Fugue means run away
run away from everywhere
or else they'll find you.

A cloud in a bikini
no kind of disguise will help,
they'll know you as I do by your fear

the way dogs they tell me can smell my fear
and act upon it as their nature bids
our common enemy, the universal bite

O the fuss a map a map can make,
ships bouncing on the sea
like syllables in Chaucer

O come home and let me sleep
warm in my mom's old sealskin   *MRK*
I told you I came from the sea.

133.
Only a pagan can revere God
truly, he knows so many,
makes up for my ignorance,

hear everything as *concerto*
strife or striving between me and them,
Spinoza and Hobbes,

naked woman and the nation state.
Mandelshtam silenced to Siberia
that east without a west, never came home.

Can you eat a flag?
Quench your thirst on law?
How has it taken us so long

to come such a short way from the start,
apple tree of Eden
still grows on this island,

stems writhing from a sea of ferns
where naked Eve is still sleeping.
I creep towards her on my belly

my flat mouth slick with questions,
philosophies, gradations,
commandments, easy songs.

134.
I bless and bless
wake with pulse beating
in the occiput that

treasure house
you call it a dream
I call it a weird hotel

where all the rooms connect
where friends who never died
come back from the dead

It turns out we all are priests
but so few of us say Mass —
most of us content to watch and grieve

how long it takes for kindness
coming through our arteries
his queendom right here

ni Mecque ni Jérusalem
a mountain in the middle of the air,
climb that, wise guy,

as we used to say when secretly
we hoped the guy was wise
and wisdom could be catching.

135.
Cracked dinner plate with good food
ornate crucifix on the epistle side
like a ladder we all must climb

word by word, bad knees,
aching ankles, the miracle
is just being here.

Here heals.
Met Bill Mullen coming down the stairs
elegant in grey tweed — is that possible? —

we sat and gossiped far away
the Mass went on,
it always does, I fled through the hotel,

bad dogs etc., but always
always a way out
of this narration.

Time to believe
time to climb the sky
rung-less as *Himmelfahrt*

the truth he is can't be far away.
Just being there is good enough.
Even better if you speak.

Because what you say
is always saying you —
does the window love me yet?

136.
Wanting a pet is slipping back from what you are.
Your loins make music,
I say music says *I do* to you enough

Schumann calling for his mother.
Or is that me?
You are enough to be and go on with,

You chose this problem for yourself
he said, but he was crying too
at all the things the self makes us do

and it's always morning, isn't it,
always what Christians call the third day.
That's why I woke

to tell you this
the words not ripe for
yet, only the tears.

137.
A humming sound like someone leaving,
windless, the trees perfectly still
out of control.

Aren't you afraid to touch old things,
won't they tinge your present
with where they've been

countless failures of the human hands
that touched this old thing?
Or is every touch a triumph

of someone speaking still?
These things make you think
thoughts long in them stored,

storied, bluebird on the hill.
A rock fell from the murdered migrant's hand,
doesn't anyone remember?

It's all a fugue and everything
has to come
again and again through all the doors.

Look out all the windows,
sleep in all the beds,
hide in the cellar and run out over and over

because that is the nature of nature
the minute you let it
turn into the oldest music.

138.
There was no music before Bach
or maybe Biber,
just people being beautiful out loud

then something happened
and beauty lasted longer than itself
and gave us to think.

There are not many roads to silence
and music is the softest of them
though the longest

with pretty girls and boys along the way,
fangless wolves and paper forests
a pirate ship in every tub

and no more war.
I touched my hand
I wondered who it was.

139.
We don't have to know all the names
but they all are blessing us at once —
what else is a name for?

I have no hero
only her
she walks through herstory

as she walks through me
because I have no story
just to be here now

and then if you let me face you
which side of the page am I on
the original or the translation?

linden flowers captivate the bees
or is it twilight on the Hellespont
already, speaking of seas

held close in the earthen arms of
it really is Poseidon owns the land
and the sea — Zeus the air, Hades the unseen.

Which brings us back to the smell of flowers,
some I listened to
some floated off on the canal

away past Santa Maria
into the narrow sea
perplexed with islands—

remember me on the white steps
waving to no one in particular
a pigeon walking through my shadow

and I dared to call all that Love
as if grapes were ripe already on the vine
and I plucked one, just one, and gave it to you.

140.
What about the miracle of standing here
or a tree full of bees?
What about water standing still?

The *absolute interior*—
that's where words come from,
they change their clothes as they come out,

weeping grenadiers,
bold adolescent mistresses
priests of Osiris or Cybele

just choose your book
use it for your pillow
and sleep the discrepancies away.

When all the subjects have come home
and the Queen is sitting on her throne
only then the fugue might end.

141.
suddenly I was in a different story
that is how it happens
this life thing, this becoming.

Casting
as if a spell or a play
or the death mask of a friend

putting something into form,
burning the dictionary,
taking the poem out of its clothes

a hundred years of French quibbling!
Sunset over Catalina Island
Thomas Mann averts his eyes

this is war
there are some things you shouldn't see
never watch what travel shows you

the only things to trust
are the weeds on your sidewalk
or the bus at the corner

or sometimes the laundromat or the moon
everything else is a deception
a snare for the greedy sensorium,

believe me, señor, there is nothing there.
When you wake in the middle of the night
and everything is still and empty and terrible

that is the truth
all the rest is memory of some book
you wrote in another life.

Humans are nothing but novelists
their stories never end
but one day I found as I said

myself in another story
you called it a dream, remember,
I called it a hotel

glass walls, would he get there
in time to save her
from the other him,

he and he hurrying, she trying clothes on
to find one at least
garment that was hers, was her

brown or green, velvet or cotton
dressed we are safe from enemies
in this story there was no dream,

confer human personhood on beasts and fish,
you think tools in the tool shed
are at least alive as the house cat or a rabbi

we are what we believe
makes most of us whores
but at least the bridges gleam in the sun

people going somewhere
you measured shadows of people passing,
sandstorm, Tartar raid — the crow warned you

but you didn't flee with all the rest
and now the city gates are shut
sun locks the end of the street and no sleep.

142.
Tell me the story that has no story —
will I get there in time to hear the beginning
since this one never ends?

Unchain the radiator, let the floor alone —
your business is with blossoming,
looking good and feeding hummingbirds —

there's that word again,
apostle? epistle? narthex, apse?
You are a building I have to search out.

I use your name but I mean someone else —
the fox who dwells beneath the pergola
teaches her cubs how to pounce

(the war never ended) (the moon still bright)
waning is winning
this is chiasmus (a man on a cross)

he claimed that night tires and daytime bores
I felt sorry for him
the way I feel for a branch that I brush in the dark

if only I could read
I would understand the night
between sleep and sleep a bardo of despair.

143.
The glass she commonly drinks water from
is blue, deep, sea at evening, a mussel shell.
But I spot five roses on the hibiscus now

or a twinge in my right flank. Facts.
Life. Abundance. Dance. You're here
with me all day long

or is it sleep? Confound the Spartans,
laze and read books, infest an island
with your soft requirements.

But not those isles of entitlement
you have to be white-born to,
leave them to new money and the Lyme ticks.

Be alone in my sea
that's how I want you
and me on every side,

every image is a malady
cured by the silences of touch.
The healer's name embedded in the rock.

144.
The revision begins before the text,
divorce planned before the meek *I dew*,
a simpering symphony,

take back the time.
They are almost close enough to be.
Through opera glasses glamorous oboist,

sighs the whole slow movement,
nobody wrote this.
I found it on the ground and hoisted it

here into the metarsia of poetry
he raved, and I listened, remembering
things have no authors but themselves,

no creator,
chalk marks on the sidewalk
blab of the pave   *WW*

I rejuvenate myself by chanting
this silly new bible spilling from my lips
as from your hips once

on a smaller sea
a wave of foam
shaped itself to shore

and Paradise began, the real one,
no murky Eden full of tests,
just the open island that is still us.

145.
We live the instant.
Everything else betrays —
how could you be tired of the rain

(it was not raining)   *SB*
what could you compare it to,
a deep blue glass of water

If I had a street
you would be living on it
yes I believe in angels

but not the kind you mean.
These walk as dream
and fill our space with their sound

sometimes I can hear as words —
I do not presume to know
if words are meant by anyone,

beautiful sunlight waiting for its prey
morning just the birds and me
hide in movement hide in speech

a kind of waterfall all round us
made of air.
Wake soon and free me from myself

another orphan clutching a spar.   *HM*
I must have come home at last
or you'd not be reading this —

and what is that strange thing on the ridge
the thing that worries you but we can't see?
A hole in reality shaped like a white fox

where the colorless otherness shows through?
I have the same thing inside me too,
let it talk its way to Paradise

which as we know just means a garden
with a wall around it.
Or maybe just the wall.

146.
You don't have to learn Persian,
don't even have to go in,
ripe pears on branches dangle over the wall,

go steal your philosophy
sleep with the girl next door.
Jouissance first repentance after,

That's the little
wisdom of the Western
lands, our chemistry.

147.
Feather of a mourning dove
petal of a funeral flower
these are the best offerings

the spontaneous, the pure.
I've waited so long to tell you this
the shrine exists so you can worship,

I heard the train again last night
there was no train where I am born
white sand Baltic coast white bathing suit,

nothing is random
how could it be?
Proust on the rue de Sevres,

you think that's an accident?
or Thomas in Travemünde
where I saw the ship

the mighty sails that make the wind blow?
I have come home to you every time—
Every image leads to the end of the world.

148.
For these are the end times
when it begins again
other side of believing

I saw the dragon lurking in the air
called out to each other
numbers in a formula

decoding us both.
And the ever-maiden in the stream
watched us carefully

she knows intimate the gospel
we have to write
half-done already and still not begun

what would you tell a maiden,
René, you who lifted   *RMR*
the names of so many

into the angelic shimmer
where the mist turns gold?
You started all this

without the least beginning.
Wild roses in a sea fog
my true love gave to me.

Cock crow up the hill
now is no time to remember
the movie is over the dream begins

the dragon was a waterspout made of pure gleam
she came from England and here I am
(fingernail clippings in a witch's pouch)

I didn't know that they were living still
Presbyterian steeple don't count the roses.
Amateur archeologists tasting dirt

small crystal into which sickness had been drawn
leave it in the stream Keekenhanna
running water carries the soul away

witches wise to cross no stream
there the leech lurks to taste your meaning
no cars overtake me I must be going very fast.

149.
On this quiet porch full of gloaming
I yearn for brisker music
but this cello's slow

her face in profile
as if on a coin
Queen of the World

if no one's there they still can see me
sustain the ebb
the whole sea could go back home

no idiosyncrasy but the word itself
how do you spell her aster
when it's still tiger lily time?

Brings back to life
chews leaf
oily root

soothe this oil along the sin
pray to the wooden horse
but jump off the merry-go-round,

arrive with upwelled ocean
servomechanism old-fashion brain
squabbling symmetries!

Bring childhood with you as you go,
grow, the truth is all you are
then the sun sat in the treetops

finch and titmouse, cardinal quick
they're really halfway between
brain and actual out there air

scenario for our tryst
moon-bathing in wane light
speaking all our needs out loud.

150.
Chew the leaf
the small quick taste
agitates the evidence

remember love before the candle dies
bright things in the market
fuel your dream she said

what makes you think
you're thinking, what
does doing have to do with being

(what are you doing today
I don't know I just remember)
the bird beats on the glass

upstart theologies,
I have a hankering for pantheon
silks and cummerbunds and nom-de-dieux

they tend to share one name
they are powers and they play in us
and from their sport our dignity, lilts on,

ode by symphony, fresco by cathedral,
you love it, they kick something loose in us
so miracles abound.

He spoke and I called him Little Priest,
priestess almost by his allusiveness
but secretly I asked What do you know of stone

how hard to carve, words to keep in line?
but to be rational oft is impolite
so I let him steer a while, just watched the sail

billow like the moon above us,
night fishermen, timid thieves
no sheriff bothers chasing

so on we coursed upon the godly sea
gods in flowing chlamys or wolf-pelt fell
we make up heaven as we go,

sometimes the moon is yellow too.
When he sneaks on his sister's clothes
and dances low over cornfields, October.

151.
Cross the bridge with me
backs to that musical hill
turn left, let it be midnight,

walk along the river,
stand. Watch the slow flowing.
Water has no place to sleep.

Lean on the parapet, close,
close, it could be Paris even
at this hour but what isn't.

Pale hulk of the museum
on its island, our arms
round each other, making sure

the other is really there.
It's not all could-be and let-be,
make sure it's simple. It is.

It was not. I was alone there.
We live in a hotel, always,
all of us, only a hotel

sometimes changing rooms
or do they only change the windows
on us, vistas vary,

the pillow warm from your own head
everlasting. How alone it sometimes is.
In the technology museum

the river flows both sides of it
all the famous engines are quiet.
Once something moved. No more.

Mystery of stillness at a distance.
Newton's unspoken dream,
that alchemist on his way within.

All I have done is say their names
each one a rung on Jacob's ladder,
each one a heaven of our standing still.

Climb me! I must have meant.
Must mean. Use me to ascend, assent,
with my last strength I hold the gate open,

the doorway that was never shut.
Agency is ominous—
we try to do the already done,

that's why it's midnight by the Isar,
the museum of the heart is always dark,
shadowy moonlight through glass roof

on curious acquisitions pedestaled on guesswork,
hope, grief. Each has a little card beside it
in ancient letters spell its name, this person

statue, figurine, full length portrait,
snapshot. And over there all my itself
Dürer's red chalk sketch of his mother.

All the rest is mine. My fault.
My greed. All differences dwindle,
grass on the lawn cut to one same height.

152.
I pressed the eject button, sent myself to sleep.
And there you are again,
lost brother, woman cousin, *inconnue*.

So many animals in my zoo
with me, and I who own the lot
live in the smallest cage.

Jone's *Bienenkorb* and we have heard her hum.　　*HJ*
He said, and I supposed the lecture ended
but I was still talking:

imagine an old-time candy store,
soda fountain, daily papers in Polish and Yiddish,
cigars on display, a soft-core pin-up

stuck to the mirror wall so you see her
when you look to see yourself.
Outside, a bleak avenue, boardwalk, sea.

Imagine this with me. Light up a Tareyton,
drink a Mission Orange from the bottle
 — no straw, suction not yet invented.

Isn't it comfortable just standing here
waiting for the war to end, begin,
take on meaning, widows in black, shopping bags?

153.
Aaron's rod feels foolish in my hand
yet I would be a priest and praise
all the living gods of earth and sea and sky

the all-pervading mind, clear light
inside light, the word inside silence
and the silence inside the word —

so put up with my antics,
every image is dangerous,
everything that is can think.

There, that should hold the Visigoths at bay —
the stone comes with you gladly
just don't dare put a price on it —

money hurts women. She told me so.
Or was it that laws hurt her money?
You decide. The case is closed.

But the mower is still educating grass —
how dare you all be different
he growls through his machine.

I sit in my summerhouse and rule the world.
Wake up and pay your taxes,
a kiss before breakfast, new-mown hay.

154.
The birds are up to something
what do they know?
We've watched five thousand years and still can't tell.

Weather changes, angry gods,
bad phone call, sprained ankle,
wolf in the woods, typo in the text

they give us all the news at once
and like the mockingbird in everybody's voice.
The business of birds!

There are no frontiers
in physics, Hakim, my friend,
or there are only frontiers —

we don't know
how the simplest thing works
really, and there are no simple things.

We forgot how to listen
and not just to the rose.
The steel bar is waiting to be heard

and the chip of mica in the schist block sings.
Manhattan stone
my mother's bones.

155.
So this is my Song of No Self
tenderly she picks the sick mouse up
and carries him outside, a baby

newborn, sick in the new world
does the house face the wrong way?
Is the king on the wrong throne?

A blue jay tried to question me
in Sealish since my mother was
how got so much ocean in his small beak?

I fret about these things
the mower sings
by eating grass he could sustain the earth

Nebuchadnezzar *ate grass like an ox*
no god and no czar
his madness was to say the truth

we are beasts and on each other feed
yet by our cruelty redeem , he said,
here, take this if you don't believe

but I was past the sweet game of believing
my cards were all torn
my dice cup empty but a spider in it.

156.
Who knows what the floor was really like
before they laid the earth on it
and the stone and all the metals rife within,

when there was just the *ground*
in chaos for the wet wind
since all water comes from breath,

hence life, hence music, hence what you say
to me in the morning, the evening
also has its anthem.

Who lives here anyhow
what is the blue light doing down the well
how can I follow so often

again and again and goes nowhere
but here where I suppose myself to be
I said, but he demurred in crimson,

blood thou art and blood returneth
whiplash of the heart
you only think you're thinking.

And then I knew he'd said that before—
I've got you now, old pontifex!
Repetition, infant, is the start of dance.

157.
do a thing once and no one cares
do it twice and music starts
lift up your trotters and beguine!

Maybe maybe rabbi bold,
I have spent my adult life
reading between the lines I studied as a child

endless epic poem
teaches us how to make gold
if we read it sideways through the door

the royal palace! king gives you his throne!
sit there eating grapes and pie
made from rhubarb and chrysanthemums,

you can't fool an American
we're born the other side of sane
and folly to the Greeks is green to us

prairies and sequoias and the corn maze
every fall, Christ I'm tired of grown-ups
they never want to learn anything

what kind of dance is that I ask you
but are you there to hear me
or are you one of them too?

I am the other Dionysus sober and sullen
in my basket are crow quills and vellum
 hard cheese made from panther's milk.

158.
When there's nothing left to argue
I offer these nano-fictions
to lead you up the stairs

each gist a lust
from which evolves
a tale of Beatrician consequence

and here we are
hobbling to heaven
long after the show is closed

but you can still hear the music echo
as once in Leipzig in Bach's church
I heard as I have elsewhere told—

o grant me intertextual permission
rising on the planes
into the soft green eyes of God.

You can tell he's near the end
he's starting to make sense
abbreviate the obvious!

The leaf covers itself with gold
I call it dawn rain birds in a bush
things that mean little last forever

lost on the railroad like Bruckner's hat
found on the shore like a baby seal
I can show you pictures of the world,

priest carrying the sacrament to a dying man.
Everything ready to begin,
sleek of tires on wet road,

magic reaches out and touches
taps you on the knee
the lower body is closer to the truth.

159.
Love prompt to kindle in a well-born heart　　　　DA
all words of mine translate that text
he never wrote but I was listening

so many versions and only one Africa
from which in their day
they saw the sun come up washing her hands.

Suddenly he knew that burden
he'd held bundled inside him
all those years was simply fear

and fear was no more than an empty sky—
unwrapped it and let the terror go,
heart lighter much, skin a little old.

All the ways a man can answer
so quick the stone in winter
heal fever now

rain soft beginning, last winter's snow
still twelve feet high by Boston harbor
we are midshipmen on a creaky hulk

no sign of a captain.
Still, we know our divers trades
but know not why we ply them,

the sails all rags or are they clouds
or are they frigate birds, mere gulls,
was that my cellphone ring or yours?

The sea has too many voices to be sure.
Suitable metaphor for all-embracing love
to be drowned or drenched at least in thee.

He closed the book, the stories
he told himself were creamier,
lasted longer, did not affright.

And overall meant less thank god,
some spirit in a handkerchief
waved from a window

thought she called my name
but it could have been anyone
and so could I.

160.
Seize opportunity to pass
from desire to desired thing
and then through it, from it, beyond.

But what is beyond
and who could it be,
low-shouldered or low-hipped

eyes busy with the fugues of sparrows,
and all our mute condensations
echo in his/her ears.

Don't ask me the gender of the real —
the dance is made of indecision
I'd be no fiddler of that tune

but play on union-pipes *The Lass of Erigal*.
No words suffice for that estrangement,
look back at the bridge and she is gone.

But we, we, slept on Tara's knoll
and came by way of faerieland
to ordinary life, yellow taxi at the door.

161.
The certainties too
are in our hands.
I am no palmist, Egyptian,

but I know my lines
as well as any spiv-sly actor,
I can see the future in the past

smashed light bulb in the wastebasket
I know the dark will come again
she'll write with candles till we see

Tell me your night tale again
the one that goes upstairs and sets the light
on again so children cry *stella, stella,*

which even in our West Dutch means a star,
a star. Here they are all round us
waiting to be astonished,

rename your constellations,
as Jordan begged you to
and blind Arthur dragoman'd for him.

So we have no excuse for not rejoicing
in the Seven Messengers, the Angel of the Middle,
the Burning Bush, the Mother and her Son.

And while you're at it
name everything all new,
here, this blank book your lexicon,

dictionary of true words yet to come.
He spoke, but I was still half asleep,
distracted by someone in the trees,

too late for Guinevere,
too warm for an owl
the stream was half-hid, though,

it runs around our house
we call it Dranse or Drench or Metambesen
fat from a month of rain.

162.
I number your paces
the steps you take to get to me
I walk the world like a sick man lying down

always anxious for the nurse to come
bringing one more dreaded elixir —
hating the thing that gives me life!

He cries out and I try to ease him,
I am no stranger to anxiety,
a pessimist by heart, green as County Monaghan,

but my ailments are the fleshly kind
and do not speak the soul,
I comforted him, stories of childhood,

root beer, videos of dragonflies,
my famous visit to the Swedish mine
where a young stone man is perfectly preserved.

I hummed him tunes from opera, brushed his coat,
wiped his glasses and set them on his nose,
and actually his world did look a little better.

There is a place for fiction in this law
haggada is halakha
(ask Philo what I mean by this)

still it wasn't anywhere near dawn.
Just me and the purling stream,
a voice thirty rods away

drunk as pigeons and far from home.
Sometimes I think I'm the last one here
but then I bother to open my eyes.

163.
They won't just let us go, you know,
we have to make our joyous exodus —
and how dare they call what they trade 'shares'

money never tells the truth —
that's all you have to know about politics.
Get money if you can, but don't believe it—

he was back on track again.
As usual, his eyes bright, words
fluent — a man happy to have enemies.

If you color outside the lines
the pictures change —
breeze runs in the window

mood changes, men merry,
altitudes of energy
hoisted by modest aerostat,

Count Zeppelin's birthday and my father's!
Jubilation and bible chanting
and watching slow from not too far above

are there still quaggas in the zoo,
I saw one once, still wild roses
on the cliffs of Oregon?

164.
Desire focuses on a blue stone.
Street lamp in the snow globe gleams,
let things do my remembering for me.

She calls her cellphone Doris and it answers
I knew a girl in Munich once,
an autumn river calm with russet leaves

names so little, men so big
shoehorn a big dream into a little sleep —
sit on the ground like foxes and look up waiting

(when all this while the moon
had not changed his posture in the sky)
not a light to see by but a light to be.

165.
There, that's what the dream was saying,
the one without words or images.
Dream a feeling of something missing

suddenly found. Not the moon this time.
Archer on the edge of the woods with longbow—
with my eyes I couldn't see her any arrows

I could sit here and hunt for dawn
comes easily these days
or sleep my way to Jericho again

where Moses' daughters run
a cunning school for love's diplomacy
and otherworldly wisdoms all combined;

they let me in some nights
let me interrogate them
in my broken Hebrew to learn how,

just how. For they know everything
again. Small school all white adobe
shadowy within, we see by skinlight,

read by the light left in our eyes
by years of looking outward.
We too are letters of an alphabet

a different one, scarce written,
no longer spoken on the earth
but you hear it, easy, in the sky.

166.
And now it's just night —
I smell an animal outside,
deer musk or raccoon,

the first people are not far away,
not their fault we see so few,
we teem with imperceptiveness,

they romp through our trees
as we think they are
because they stand in dirt we claim to own.

167.
Vital to turn the will away from wanting
otherwise you end up with everything,
but not the one right thing

your heart most needs.
You know that after hours spent with friends,
the missing feeling the when-will-it-end.

Dissolve all wants in will
and let the one thing quietly approach,
suddenly there, Magi from the east

and you just newborn of your will.
That's one thing the story means,
O shepherd without a single sheep.

168.
Thing we fear
not different from we are,
stamens and pistils everywhere you look

so he finally took
(perceived) the world as
a flower (why not?)

the bridges were empty
but in mind's eye thronged
with rush hour traffic from years ago

all these black cars and meek police.
But time is broken now
and he is left remembering,

his thoughts climbed aboard a yellow bus
and went to school
a whole day free to share boredom,

delicious vacancy of other people's books
looks blackboards questionings,
cool breeze on a muggy day.

No sweat. Pledge allegiance
to attention, but never tell
on what Grail your attention's fixed.

169.
The Quest is quiet to begin.
Event means outcome or coming out
or watch how the wind blows

go alone but take me with you
there's always an Other on a solitary quest
lead mines of Gallatin, silver on your shoe

once I was a pirate too
I mean I lifted dead leaves from the stream
cherished the architecture of what is left

after time got broken and went home.
More than you need to imagine
less than you could

the Wizard said, the man who once meant wise.
A mighty furnace roaring at his heels
or is it Smilodon my cat

yes, they can talk,
it's our fault we can't hear them.
When they sleep they dream our thoughts in us.

Yes, I am an alchemist
but I wear clothes and walk along the street,
lost in thought like everybody else.

170.
The shape of it shimmers before you now
reach out and touch it
don't be startled if it feels like skin

for of ourselves all things are made
caress the girders of the being-built
kiss the window on the hundredth floor —

who could it be but you or me?
The pananthropic principle,
it's all made of us

only we are made of something else.
Ban the book.
The mind is your mother.

171.
Raptacious she said
and I became,
long slope of back

the curt of hair—
blossomly living
glass full of water only

miracle of senses—
my green eyes wait for thee
it said in church.

Heavy traffic on the overpass
I huddled under, a troll I was
and my trolless with,

kept warm by friction
of the water roughing over our skins—
movement is heat

the church said that too,
willingly wandering
house in his head

always at home
because I roam—
rub that off the blackboard

nobody has to know
how easy it is to be,
the new day needs

an empty word
to soothe the strangeness
of the nothing there.

I tell myself these stories all the time
until they come true
by speaking in you.

One day I woke up
in a strange part of my house
a room I never knew

someone moved
beyond the wall,
I heard voices but not words

just as I to you today
to tease inside you out
a word you never heard.

172.
In the street of strange bodies
will I sense her approach?
What happens when we're someone else?

Can you still find me?
Isn't some music leading
space all the time?

Come sit with me and mend my story
it needs you in it,
person from the stone,

the lake sinks into the rock
a starboard sun tries to overcome
but grey crested birds bring on the night.

I see the lapis clutched in your hand
and want to touch it to my brow.
And my eyes too have need of stone.

173.
I met Francesca there again,
she seemed tired of not dying.
But it is not death that keeps you young

I claimed to ease her, you can pause
your circle anytime you choose,
a circle leaves you anywhere

it is not a road it is a will,
another's will but can be yours,
desist from wanting and have everything!

I promised, and she listened sagely,
she has heard so much advice before
so all my wisdom smiled upon her lips

beautiful still as innocence lets anyone be,
she didn't answer me at first, and then
Will you too fall lifeless when you see

how willingly I am another's will
and he is mine, and love
has nothing to do with time

or roads or wheels or getting
anywhere, we always are —
and being is a luminous agony.

174.
So that's what the birds
were saying all this while
we are, we are

the people that you knew,
we could not meet now
if we had not met before.

175.
Leave the dream in dreamland
let it do its work
un-daylighted by doubt.

A dream is an investment —
amortize, don't analyze,
pay off your debt by deed.

What you do in the day
is all translation,
all law begins in story

stories you tell yourself
this fairyland you reckon waking.
Ferlie is *gefährlich*, dangerous.

Let me live by etymologies
the stream outside our house
words change as they flow past —

my great love would be to find
a law so great it would be
a day-long delight to obey.

Compliance is sensual,
it's being with rivers
it's riding time's back

and being friendly with the night.
I hoped I was listening,
dawn a spasm of gentleness

pale through trees —
the witches have done their work again
and foiled the bosses a few more hours,
224

look around, look all around
they whisper, watch us
rinse into the sky what is not color yet

watch and do nothing but be.
All these footnotes and no text, yes
merry-go-round for you but no horses on it.

176.
Run by theme
and hope by habit
the fugue will get you home

but who listens,
the phoebe and the cardinal
welcoming the light

who did they think I was
moving at a window
where their world ends?

A lot of it's about sleeping and waking
we'll go on like that
till we figure it out, fugue it through,

and that's the Last Judgment
and get to be awake all the time
in some neighborly eternity.

North into the light!
As if I knew which way is up,
as if light also had a habit of me.

177.
Be out there with it
the whirled space
in radical bewilderment

so beautiful on every side
in tints of flesh and green
and blue all over

be there with it to defuse
its dream, use the hard
rock of Milarepa maybe

if I'm able. But systems,
systems everywhere,
all analogy, no etymology.

We don't know where things come.
And the how of whom!
The larks of lust! Trembling aspens

on the way to the sea, tremuloïdes!
Perpend your exclamations,
raver. The town hall is open,

pointless documents amassing,
would you add to these?
I would — no telling where the told can go.

178.
And heaven ever after. So keep
these pages close to your heart.
Good insulation winters,

like the poor men of my childhood
shirts stuffed with the *Daily Mirror*.
And this also is today

and maybe ever always.
Like waiting for us in Arles
two thousand years one

girl playing a harp,
or tiny inchworm
humping along a written page.

179.
I asked the surgeon
so she said Don't ask me,
there is a star rules such matters

old Persian name
in an abandoned constellation
with bloodshot eyes,

for a month I am forgiven
that mean moon-man
the shells of love

scattered on heaven's pave
two birds before dawn
equaling a glass of wine

headache like a small red car
there are no fish in Jericho
I take my little cap off though

the lily needs nothing from me,
only water from that well
a book we sparingly believe.

180.
We learn
everything from books,
nothing from birds,

there is a reality but who knows —
maybe the names of things
are enough for a while

our little while,
anthropocene interval
— am I an intermission

you may well ask.
The sky gets brighter
are you even helping it?

We live in the age of names —
sticks and stones will break our bones
and names will surely kill us

because there is no answer to a name,
it deals a fatal silence.
It says John.

But what about words on the other side of a name
they name an action or a thing,
isn't it fatal to say arise or a rose?

Thinking crash-lands in a name —
but something slithers from the wreckage,
free from depiction, beyond the boundary,

a hint, a yen, a glint, a go.
And it begins to know.
Call it yellow or call it gold

it flees you, miser, and your avaricious dictionary
where I have said all this before.
Let those finches sleep.

181.
Apologize for not being with me —
being with is all the be we have,
the gift of not being someone else,

the sacrament of hanging around.
What else is music for?
And here I am.   *AB*

Time is crossing its fingers
telling us lies,
you also have to learn how not to listen

that too is music's tool.
Tiresome flat passages
just shut the door—

the ears have no eyelids,
go against nature
teach them to sleep

(noises in the forest,
picus, remember Mary,   *MB*
woodpecker at the heart,

the bird the heart is
she meant, battering
non-stop at something

only the heart knows
and never tells
and we keep guessing at,

like a tune we can't remember
how it goes
or what word comes next

from the abyss of what we mean
in a world of changes changing
only attention is any use.

That bird again
never stops
worrying the wood.

Input and output the same.
The system.
The fish swimming in the sky.

182.
The rosary is rotary
the child observed
one bead after another around and around

so praying equals making circles,
sending them somewhere
and making more circles again —

this is what they teach in schools
but why do they speak of roses,
he asked, no rose ever comes again.

I think dear love
it is a Buddhist epic
a poem without a self

may the stream of thoughts
arise as meditation,
that effortless clarity so hard to find

where what arises
feigns to be music
and takes you in because you hear

as Plutarch expounds at length on Plato
mad at poetry, keep it from the young
exactly because it is beautiful

when it should be calm and accurate
and even true, true as can be —
but there again I wasn't listening,

or as the Captain said,
you're a good guy, Woyzeck,
but you have no morality.

I defend my isle of allurements
until she comes to me saying
leave the island to its lake and come home.

That's why I call it a fugue
it's all about running away
or would be if only

I knew where away is.
Everything is always right here —
then why am I hungry?

Now I'm caught
the sun is in the trees,
I shrink back to my stone.

Please be near me when silence wakes
I don't know how to walk that way alone,
silence needs so many hands.

183.
Voices where none ought be
does there have to be a reason,
snow globe beside a triptych Mother of God?

The range is infinite
the grasp minute —
was that a monkey in that window?

Can it be a road if nobody goes?
Learn to write first with invisible ink
to lure the sympathetic reader —

later learn to read the lines
as if they were between themselves
or a raft on the Amazon

where it's so wide you can't see its banks
but only sense that somehow
this flow too is shaped and you are held.

184.
Sun full of trees
she wears our clothes today —
market day in mind.

Self— maybe
if I can't get rid of mine
I can get rid of its.

The raisin and the reason
sheets of Manhattan
French word in Irish mouth

and voilà! we are veiled
in hearing, wiped clean
by listening, écoutez!

It is time to dissemble again
pretend we didn't hear the tocsin
money rattles on its way to war

what if there had been no Athens
then and now, no Plato,
no Sophocles, and all we know of love

is what the Bible doesn't teach us
hammer of the heart anvil of the loins
and dakinis who flirt with us in dream,

what if we'd gone right from Babylon to now
in one long heave of oiled brutality —
would we be so different from we are?

185.
I pointed straight up
Axis Mundi ! I cried
she laughed with her furled parasol

upright, whirled and sang away off
kept singing later when I caught up
laughing wet with singing

no song I knew no words I recognized
I only knew her happiness
led her to a boulder

or was it a tree stump petrified—
this was the only guide I found
when I couldn't find my room

all the floors had changed
graduate students plied their arts
messily on every floor

and they too were joyous
helpful and brave
the way art has to be

but who was I, my office lost
between the floors
an elevator opened halfway up

so many verticals
in all her laughing
she pointed to where my place must be

another north and far away
where no building is
but she was here

and I was burdened with my history
books documents mail a sense of self
time to leave all that behind

then find your space
and there she stood drenched with singing
a woman from the middle of the stream.

I woke and staggered up the hall
drunk from what I had beheld,
confusion calm as sunlight on the lawn

so quietly the fugue came back.
A theme comes back
takes all its meaning from returning

amor fati and love what happens
happens to you
the way music does

listen as it happens
no choice,
her parasol pointed to the hub of creation

the central Tree no one has ever seen
and we all are. The rain
ran down her silver wrist (it was not raining).

186.
Every human has two
human enemies
the family and the state.

The Grail quest
aimed to be free of both,
to find the Castle of Between.

Every monster in the book
is one or other, Grendel
is the family, Humbaba is the state:

Gilgamesh reigns in Uruk,
Enkidu, "the dutiful
son" dies in the woods.

All tragedy explores
these iron gates around us,
Kafka's country doctor

looks into the wound
a flower opening —
the body

is sometimes an answer,
the answer, sometimes
that too is Grail,

Christ quest,
leading a hunan
beyond beyond

into the actual.
Here
endeth the lesson.

240

Sorry I woke
with the truth
in my teeth

had to spit it out
here to you,
blessing you for my sneeze.

187.
No punctuation darling
it's so overdetermined
nothing lost between the words

let them breathe themselves.
As in a chapel
no gap between the building and the Cup,

you drink the architecture too,
see it quivering on the skin of wine
in the moment before you sip

the stone too is a sacrament
and the work of human hands,
take all this in

be healed by it
the Grail that every morning comes
but only if you look for it

all your life till you forget
you're even looking
then it comes to you

tröstet und hilft, says Rilke
which in our ears says
trusts us and heals.

188.
Let me be quiet a while
with my other self,
the one the sun comes

to lick my other skin,
it's all in Virgil,
Melville, Dickinson,

in fright or lust
it runs to us
we laugh and say that's natural

because it so terribly is.
Then was a wall
our warrior

and a door a maybe friend.
And all birds are messengers
but are all messages the same?

Don't play your radio out the window
the silence is noisy enough,
trees have come closer to the house.

Each step a parapet
(he's scared again),
(he totters on the walls of Troy,

the lost city by Shandaken)
let language firm his steps,
alliteration is the mother of Achilles.

Language calls us and we come to be —
is that enough explanation
or are there Christians in the house

who need a Bible reference?
Then look up into the blue sky
like the apostles in *Acts*

and see what draws him up
brings down your destiny —
the next person you meet is an angel

always. Always.
The road doesn't know any other way to go.
Has to bring us together.

Here I am back to my roses
(rose stands in for any thing)
do they know I need a shave?

Do they know anything at all about me
these words that speak me?
Maybe I am no more than what they know,

know by saying?
That's why I look to the rose to
console me and help   *RMR*

rose here means any actual thing
O rose explore me with your magic lips
for example means Sun shine on me.

(And this rose is really a hibiscus
here, someday I'll get it right —
the skin is the longest disease,   *JC*

surface of the evident
we bury in the heart
the place so deep no wine can reach
244

absurd to call it organ meat
and yet the blood goes in and out
and that's all we are—

is there life beyond oxygen?
seems such a simple thing to ask
the temples come crashing down

isn't that what Samson was
a blind man's question
that broke the building down,

say the word and the city falls.
You go to a surgeon to get something out
go to the movies when you can't see enough,

why do you write me the letter you do
if not for the only answer I ever have?
Write the words down and follow them home.

189.
I'd call all this Atlantis
but Atlantis doesn't like to be talked about,
it's still there, still speaking,

you hear its gong from beneath the sea   *AN*
in every woman's hips
the first city comes to us again.

Never mind what ocean it drowned in
(a sea of angry men),
just listen, the primal sutra reads again.

190.
And the sun rains on us—   AD/EP
that's not me, that's poetry
the old man said,

everything I ever said is wrong
but not the words,
the words are always right.

You never know the distances
love must travel,
those who dare to speak of love

as if we all know what it means
yet have to be told
over and over again

by voices plodding through time
soft as marimbas
in a beastless jungle

or do I mound up misery here
like a pre-teen stuffing hankies
in her not-yet-needed bra?

but the bird is going off already
not yet light
and makes me doubt my doubt

the way natural things always
reassure us on the way
though they too know where that road goes

birds roads light things words
so little matter to so much mind
i.e., by music alone we seem.

Then things turn
out to be gone.
A smidgen of silver

to misspell the morning
and Monday is.
This is Bible stuff.

Yet sometimes in the cool of the evening
I almost wish I could see him walking
the one we thought he was once

when we were just about to be born.
There is no home
tenderer than myth

the word we heard
that meant us to move
till god knows where we are

he said, and by now
I was tired of his sermon
but who am I to interrupt

and would he even pause to listen?
Open any door
and the sea rushes in,

language full of mist,
you can feel the damp on your skin
fresh between the unsayables.

191.
Tiger day in a week
to help you think about the state
that big Other Thing that bothers us —

Who made it? nobody knows
but Engels tells, what can we do?
we affirm it every moment of the day

every time we say *we* or *they*.
I say change the language, change the basics
but Stalin says I'm wrong

(nobody knew more about state and wrong).
These are simple toys we play with,
having opinions and saying them

loud to one another,
discourse of society,
finches clamoring at dawn.

Note how they grow quiet when full light comes.
Woman chained to the cloud.
Man chained to the falling rain

(it was not raining)
holding it up to the light
we see through and see someone inside

that is the person we meant all the while,
when all the new names people have
kept fooling us

only one name for the lot of them
— deer with wet pelt gleams up the lawn —
have I made this matter clear

he said, Yes I said, clear as matter ever is.
O you and mind he groaned
this is not a dialogue it is a vine

what we say comes round and round again
what you keep wanting to call a fugue
but they all fled long ago

and where's your fugue
with no subjects to flee?
In this state every man is king

he raved, and I wept for lost music.
We are built of false etymologies
and by analogy shape what passes for truth.

(I thought I'd tell you the colors have come back,
the spectrum makes us silly sometimes,
I get excited when I see blue)

A touch subtractive
takes something from your skin
that you don't need and I can use,

how do you use it I wanted to know—
it turns into a special air inside me
that makes the words that answer you now.

In other words I form
with anyone I touch
a perfected system to express

something neither of us knows.
Mesmer never touched his patients
I protested, yet they were healed.

192.
Paradox of seasons
we begin where others end
always a first time again

and Shakespeare is the only one who could,
trusted language to know what he could not
self-educated by the word itself

or when I touch you
do you want (do you mean)
it to be another hand

other side of me, the paragon,
paramour, paladin, *inconnu*?
So why not Shakespeare,

why not let him write his plays
and you write yours,
be better, be genius,

then look down on that drunken hick
our master.
And who ever came from Nazareth anyhow?

193.
Bird-harping cool mist morning
I rest my case
in the actual, or what seems so,

for what do I know
except what gives itself
touches me too with their famous hand?

Wake up and tell lies?
Be angry at the obvious?
Homer's Troy is somewhere else

Shakespeare wrote the Bible   *(Ps. 46)*
Call no man great who leads you into war —
the more they murder the bigger they loom

in the cheap PR scam called history.
Abhor them, shame them,
tear down their flags.

194.
Listless lexicon of everyday,
wash the dishes and wash the stars,
sometimes voluptuous archipelagoes.

Be near the weather
your tutelary spirit
bodies out as rain

wherefore all seasons
are manifestoes
of that being-power

To be hard and vague at once
like a princess to her tutor
teach me music if you love me

I have no need of luteless facts
fit for the sausage-maker's daughter
not for my neat hands.

195.
And all I have to do is this,
I am a Russian poet you never heard of,
I walk by the sea on Brighton Beach

where I was born this time at least
learning to talk softer than its waves
and almost make sense but never quite.

Sing lovesick lepers on the strand
body all finished except for pain
no feeling left but feelings

and now the incurable brain begins
insatiable longing serenading
all the things they cannot touch,

it is not a little thing to be unclean,
compared to, to what, what are we,
Comparing lovelorn-ness to leprosy

might make sense when you're fifteen.
But youth is boring too, all those urges,
so few dragons, maidens shy unchain you,

miser of your feeling, *misellus*, a leper,
 little wretched one, whose name in the plural
gives our 'measles', you read it on the skin,

not allowed to read, bad for the eyes,
stayed in a dark room and look at me now.
My life story in less than a sentence,

history too just a tattered fever-chart
there is no doctor left to read,
but still this Slavic ocean soothes.

196.
The wield of want
shifts through the trees
patches of sunlight

clouds must move.
I felt the grass
beneath my feet

and knew this place
again, how strange
to be here

place I call mine
all these years I barely know.
Long since I walked on my lawn.

The old indoor philosophy again   JM
kept me in after school,
then the sea freed me

and still I'm someone else
till now.
Now is soft and wet and green,

now is shadow, sun-flecked trees,
some cars go by,
not a sheep for miles.

And still the shepherd shifts
syllables to formulate
mind's inward animal in an outward world.

The sun eating an orange behind the church.
The cloud
from which we speak —

how precious the sky is,
it keeps us safe,
the trolls in us can't handle it,

all the cars roasting in the moonlight
for all you know sharing the same dream.
Be different. Look up and dissent.

Nothing lasts up there,
the words dissolve in mind
and we are water meek again —

he was running out of steam I guessed
morality is a sick man's crutch,
be quiet, reverend, while I eat my prayers.

197.
I told him I was in love
with the glimmer of the actual
the glands of light and laps of dark

through which I claim, or language
claims in me, to see the real.
He sighed away and left me to be wrong

I have a soft spot for reality I admit
and really all my dreams are part of it —
there is no gap inside between —

or if there is we fill it with our breath.
Hence mantra, music, the non-stop hum
inside the head just stop to listen —

not to speak of the catbird outside.
Glorious animal of everything!
Forgive my gush, my levee broke

your steamboat came, you rescued me —
spem in alium, my hope is in the other   *TT*
and all the voices coincide in yes.

The phone rang, now who am I?
Grass was nimble, feet slow,
from the north Achaeans came

trailing their history in disguise
as long ago the secret scribes
in Israel wrote bible backwards

so we at last could learn to read.
Adam out of Eve, Cain struck by Abel
banished to a far place called humanity

music and thingliness and cities
and there we rested till some
overbred Egyptian prince

led us through the desert
to meet a big voice on a mountain
who would not show his face.

That's what the phone said
while I was thinking about the nice wet grass
and what was that tree thinking of

when it tried to make me think
another kind of person stood there,
waved to me and vanished in the green.

198.
The Æther Principle
light turns into air
in contact with our living rock

where language is the sea
in which we travel
and light lets us breathe

by the membrane of our lungs
we lower the light to oxygen
to send light through our blood

all the dark destinations of our meat.
And so we run around the lawn and flap our arms
do strenuous things we think will help

but reading as we deeply know
is a form of breathing—
those who do not read grow weak,

soon old, miss the *answering other*
a page is rife with, or a word even
spoken through the air (the light)—

it makes us live. Technically, the *aither*
enters the *metarsia*, cools down
an octave into gaseous form,

a concert of nitrogen and oxygen
with other voices obbligato
and as aforesaid lets us live.

And if we had no language
no man could breathe
but women may have another source.

199.
Can we be red
and not be blood,
Shakespeare wrote Shakespeare

but Georg Cantor thought otherwise
he beyond the numbers numbers
thought Bacon did it

and he was wrong but right to be wrong,
because if there are transfinite numbers
there are transfinite facts —

begin by doubting what everybody knows,
crack consensus open
and see what still holds

he must have thought
as Kimberly Lyons and Joseph Summer
think Edward de Vere wrote *Hamlet,*

and did Melville think so too,
his Starry Vere captain of his final ship?
Not beyond conjecture   *TB*

their motto, don't believe
what everybody says
and just by doing so you're halfway home.

But home might be a strange place —
for all my loves are Lesbians
and I would have it so

to turn back from any *natural thing*   WBY
and soak the sky with bleaching doubt
and see if any sun comes out,

that ordinary thing by which we live.
Maybe Mexico was right,
there is a black sun beyond the white,   *JR*

the yellow thing. The truth.
So Cantor must have reasoned
there is a truth beyond the truth

but I've gotten all this wrong.
This is just machinery inside my fugue
the animal that scurries behind the garage.

Clandestine marriages, births unregistered,
dowries paid in kind, a witch in a tree,
we are three: the lie, the truth, and it,

beyond the implications of roses or the smell of words.
In saddle bags they brought it from the East
but when we tore them open it was gone.

200.
So the other side is Nowhere Else
at the end of numbers there are only words
propositions are the roses lost in leaves

but god the bare branches are beauty too
and the leaves la-la before the rose —
only paulownia flowers first

purple gauds, bare monkey puzzle tree —
sunrise in the graveyard, the Rights of Man.
I was in a place I knew before

all the animals left me alone
but there were people in the leaves
who waited to see what I would do.

I sat on a fallen tree in that dark place
and pretended to read
a book I pretended to hold in my hands

but here I read out loud to you.
There is a little window in the ground
you see clear glass inside the turf,

shows the beginning of a quiet road
kneel down and see the moon in there
watch him totter down the dark

where everything can be said
beyond all accounting,
little hole in your own ground—

is there a transfinite language too
where sentences we can't think
wait for us in some image?

nonsense leaps from our lips
must, because sense led nowhere.
All we have to do is end the war.

On the table, words moving around,
numbers, shark teeth, syllables,
letters from the landlord, hands.

201.
My I is like Dante's:
I was never there
I am not now,

I'm just some grammar to hold your hand
lead you through images
stories that never happened.

the mighty city no one ever saw,
the sea that speaks pure language
and the mountain that at last is silent.

Exemplary distinctions
approximate the physical gulf
between right thigh say and left

of someone walking uphill
fast, the vee-ing, the scissoring
limbs of such ascent—

measure it.
Tell it to me
while the didjeridu's hollow clamor

opens the waste places
and someone comes.
Sounds come from things.

Hylonoesis. Things have minds.
All minds can talk.
and out come the bodies

of beasts and men, all
language of the elements
at play. Play.

There are no accidents
and every seeming has its sense,
agreed? Evening mist on the Yamuna,

the people of religion
will be busy with the night.
The electricity cuts out about now,

prayer flags calm down over the gardens.
I heard nothing I could understand
but that's not unusual with me.

To hear is to profit from mistaking.
It is now everywhere!
the child realized

and shut his picture book
but kept a finger in it
at the page where the stone gives milk.

202.
Let it be morning
the gyroscope has been spinning   *TP*
quietly its night web around the earth

and this prism we see through
this angled atmosphere
starts from the horizon

to do its work again.
How did you know I knew
light turns into breath?

You were ready, and it is hard
to be ready for what happens
but we always are.

203.
Just give me bone
to bear all this meat
this cloud that vagues vision

may have been Nebraska last night
or something you found along the way
a grammatical convenience

or otherwise, a rutilant crystal
dropped on those stairs
that don't lead anywhere

but they have both foot and head
al som del escalina   *AD/DA*
like anybody else.

Seems lunacy to me
to spend your days
going up and down the staircase of yourself,

gymnastic delirium. But to do it,
Valéry cautioned, armed to the teeth,
lunacy. Better be hollow.

Hollow Earth theory should really mean
there is nothing inside the body,
just a central sun peopling vast emptiness.

204.
I knocked on my door
there was nobody home.
Just the light outside

I stood a while among it
considering (holding a star
in my hand to help me think)

decided that whatever happened
I would tell you all of this,
a word feels better spoken.

Maybe the stairs are all behind me now
maybe I'm upstairs already—
it's the window problem all over again:

you can't be sure ever
if you're looking in or looking out.
No windows at Çatal Höyük, none in the kiva.

Sun in the trees not there before.
I trust the evidence but not the senses.
In the kiva we carry light down with us,

a man is not transparent
has just two little eyes way up on him
so let a house have a hole in its head

they said and locked the roof against danger—
could they have thought the enemy was light itself?
Sit in the dark and remember.

To speak and not speak at once
is best, to say it and not say it
and flee by night from all the things you meant.

205.
Counting time in the world
is hard on the thumb—
keep that bobbin spinning

Mani-khor, a wheel that prays
and makes the room around you
vibrate with assent.

You gave me the skeleton of a leaf   *CMK*
those veins are bones
everything intact yet we see through

this is my body
I want to say
past all the obscure meanings of the flesh

fat with signifiers
amateurs of sunrise
always glad of Anything More

yet the gothic austerity of this leaf
shall be my teacher from this hour
how does it happen

to be so clear
and every part distinct
the whole form perfectly complete—

an image is all I could ever mean.
Just because the light is there
do I have to run out and be with it?

I am a triptych closed upon myself
propped above a curious altar
in a chapel of the indeterminate,

all kinds of religion chant around me
but who am I?
You have to come to the altar, reach over it

open me up
and whatever you exclaim
will be my name,

that's what every I needs
from every you, *capisce*?
as we used to say in the Old Mill

when as I child I used to wonder
why other people were.
By now I almost know.

206.
Whose fault is language anyhow
and why do we keep saying what we see?
Is seeing never finished till it's said?

Children shouting names in the backseat
car going through blank landscape
we have to make exciting or we die.)

I have no right to tell you this
you have every right to listen.
We are whistle-blowers on reality

and we pay the price,
Mahler every summer a new symphony
or making love to whatever happens,

glass ball on a window ledge
coincidentia doesn't mean coincidence
it means a marriage.

Let the instrument explain itself
probing the avenues in wood
or just slicing the envelope

so all the words bleed out
till we are virgins again
or always were

and the books just tell lies
about us and all things.
Time has not even yet begun.

207.
Why are some people born too big?
To teach them they don't fit in,
they'll have to work hard to find their place

and never will, the flower
is bigger than the leaf,
they'll waste their bigness

on learning to be small
and never will. It is wrong
to fit in, fitting in

is normal, is natural, is disaster.
So why are some people born too small?
To teach a similar contradiction,

they'll work hard all their lives
to be big and never will, they forget
the bird is smaller than the sky.

Escape the consequences. Born big
or born small, it is your *genius*
building you out and out and out

from the thought you are. I, Paul,
a citizen of Rome,
tell you this, *do not conform*

to the system, but renew instead
your first mind.
The mind that makes you

He paused, perhaps overburdened
by the truth he'd spoken,
or by doubt. He hunched over the counter,

his bony shoulders sharp in old tweed.
How long have we been wearing this world
I asked him, expecting no answer.

He stared into the blue fire
beneath the grill where a counterman
was being deft with hens' eggs. Over easy

I think I heard her stipulate
the woman in the booth behind us
her cellphone propped in the silk flowers.

Why do we sit beside one another?
How many years have we been on the way?
Coming here? And why is food?

208.
Can't but won't. Leave space
for air, for getting there.
I read the letter that you wrote

I was in the city then, entitled
to the language of the place. Now
I don't know. No wonder I think trees talk.

But your letter took most of the world away,
you didn't tell us what comes next —
you hinted, but I could sense your own uncertainty.

It is all about uncertainties he said —
they give us energy to choose for ourselves
what picture of reality we credit,

that feeds the mighty energy called faith.
Faith to lick the honey of uncertainty,
to catch the gleams of sky through foliage.

But we were in a diner with no leaves,
the grill now empty, the woman eating —
I could hear her knife and fork dance on her plate,

sarabande of slow breakfast. She drank tea.
Beside me he was speaking, quoting something
in what sounded like Greek. Or a problem

in mathematics. A swan on a little lake.
A tow truck on its way to be of help,
a newspaper under his elbow.

What did you just say? Nothing much,
I was remembering my first love,
a boyish girl in Smyrna, hoyden you'd call her,

we courted in bad Greek,
she died of some disease that women get.
I was just saying the syllables of her full name.

Enough fiction! I want pure lies,
me to thee, all the gush
I hope comes true.

I wanted to leave this dive alone —
follow my own shadow on your pavement,
walk quick away from any voice at all

but whichever way I went
there'd be a bird or frog croaks in a pond,
things are always talking,

209.
I think all I am is one who hears,
bad ears, bad eyes, and it never stops talking.
I rest my glance on my shadow how quiet it is.

I am a dark place after all
a raft of sinning
glib on the tropic estuary

no banks in sight, just you—
that was you in your other language
woman in a web of other people's meanings —

such a familiar tragedy,
see why I trust only the body to be true?
We knew each other on that raft

and why they call it Amazon.
Breastless, unmothering, very strong.
Dolphins swim a hundred miles upstream.

And we are animals also,
fleet of fear, trusting hair and horn,
dum amo vivo

take love away it all goes wrong.
Any kind of love? You betcha —
what's wrong is right.

210.
 We left of course together
the diner and stood in the parking lot
discussing spiritual geometry

whatever that is,
about which he had a lot to say.
I watched the sky

the way I always do,
such a miracle, the empty set,
the signless sign.

And full of light,
all of it on its way to us,
automatically, spontaneous,

like a kid running
out into the year's first snow.
Of course I was happy.

The real kind
that becomes the mind
no sorrow can take away.

And there was silence
in the sky
for half an hour

and I knew he had finished
whatever it was
he thought I had to say.

Enough of saying
sing some
for the nice lady little

boy who loves the crannies
the clefts, meek geology
of anyone you choose

to use as target,
trouvère, to your tune—
go tell us love

is like this and like that,
a cushion on the stone   *poikilothron...*
where only on this earth

true lovers can meet,
seat on the shore of the little lake
we call infinity.

211.
To be deceived by unity
in the act of counting,
courting. I remembered

the feel of the man beside me
as he spoke of her
the first love, the way

a crystal shatters, or quieter
the way a prism breaks the light —
love is like that, all analysis.

I mean love between two people
he insisted, not some vague
be-nice-to-everybody-ness

I mean the hard kind
the alchemy,
shark tooth, lamp in the window,

catbird, empty fridge,
out all night,
the hair dye fading.

Why are you old
I asked him, why not tree,
motorboat, scalpel,

why not spirals, why not code?
But he was gone before my list of exceptions
ended, it could never end,

in this world of ultimate forgetting
I need simple as a reflection
in an upstairs window,

suppose there really was a Noah's Ark
and you are it, wandering in darkness,
waiting for your raven to come back —

then unload your lusts and angers,
your special language on an innocent rock,
everybody comes back to life.

The news channels never notice,
I don't want to walk on the ground
that's what I'm saying just listen

elevator aqueduct darning needle bird
I want to be *over*—
the form does not matter or rather

the form is the flight itself.
The fugue folds its hands in prayer.
A crow crossed the sky

why are you waiting for me
are we married?
Can it happen that way too

wed by a glance
linked by suppose?
Hummingbird, friend I know you not

there is a shape inside you that I know
I saw her once in Jericho
tall, white flowing cotton, wind

her eyes were sad
her words were glad
do you think this is some stupid song?

280

212.
Freedom to refuse is what I never had.
Storm at sea,
the chorus shouts blows the door open

I thought it was love but it was mist on the shore,
people fussing in the garden
but I love what grows by itself

amor fati he said and vanished —
everybody thinks he's a magician!
I wandered myself back to the sky.

For there is anger in the human world
and hymn tunes don't help
need a bolder potion,

ah, I have made a mousetrap for the moon
that leaves us free
for alternate alchemies galore

next year I'll catch the sun
and pin her to the door —
why not, it's the house that speaks, not me

the occupant is occupied —
what do birds remember?
time to lift the pen, and see

see what the ink says by itself —
I'm writing in twentieth century Russian
it comes out American now

who lost my watch?
Who watched me grovel in the music,
liminal infatuation

give me only the edges of things
you can have the rest,
only the hollow outline for me,

only the shape of what it could mean —
how pale the haunches of the morning —
yes trees I think it will rain.

213.
The word runs down the slope
slips over the edge, falls
to the next plane inclined below

keeps going, falling, arriving, rolling
till we turn away —
no way for a word to stop.

Every now and then a rhyme reminds.
Spelling is a chessboard
the other always wins,

the triptych opens
the Blessed Mother tells us what her Son told her
but she had whispered it to him in a dream —

how could a word be?
It's all true till you say it,
only then comes doubt,

persecution, *Mayflower*, raw tyrannies,
dead natives, steamboats, submarines,
men on the moon, assassination of everybody.

None of that is what the Mother meant.
Go back to school and learn a better alphabet,
leaner, less explicit, like the stars.

214.
Now I know where I have been,
from sleep I bring you waking,
from words a silence focused diamond's gleam.

The fugue is finished now
find another way to go on,
woman walking through the timid surf.

What could be simpler than to say?
Random teachings from the Book of Night,
the poor man has to make up his dreams himself —

any leaf outside's a letter of her name
but which leaf comes first?
Just tell me who I'm talking to

after that the ascent is easy.
I have seen mountains I never climbed
but the converse is more relevant,

a plate full of darkness and mist
I earned by great effort,
share with me now a little taste of it.

Paul again, always lost, always making sense
as if that mattered so much —
freedom comes when no one listens,

keep to yourself
the thing you thought
the symphony said.

Don't hide in history
the animal you are —
just give them what they need,

those others, as much as you can spare.
This isn't Sunday this is decency,
you have it because you're here, but so are they.

No, Walt he has it wrong again —
there were 28 maidens sporting
naked in that cool lake

and I the cold widower
who watched them from the sky —
I was the moon

and they were my phases, faces,
fancies, moods of my machine,
my aspiration, my despair.

I used what hands I have
to stroke them as they frolicked,
they are mine but I can't have them,

they speak only to each other
and to men, their half-conscious votaries,
their toilsome worshippers below.

I cannot touch what is my own —
that is the moral of my jingle,
I fall hopeless down the sky

trying to remember when I am.
The who of me is lost
long ago, maybe Plutarch knew me

but I can't read,
I am the Sun's bad eye,
her feeble squinter

I gaze on my beautiful phases
as well as I can —
at least I set them free to dance

for you, you ancient enemy my friends.
You have them, and you call them me or mine,
but all I ever had I gave to you.

215.
Rain as you come in
lambs for the daughter
flee where you please, there's only one country

and so we are far.
I heard the moon
bleating his despair.

Everyone makes love
in his light but not he,
le veuf, unmarryable, remote

and close at once. I think of him
as a piece of us, of me,
the cold observer, opal in the sky

who at his full lifts all our moisture up
as if to bathe again in what we are.
Or what he was.

Triste night, caravan of sorrows
drifting slowly past us
phase by phase we do the best we can —

this grief he teaches me to moan.
The moon. But I have work to do,
petty as suits my capacity

to live another day on earth and be of use.
Come to the temple and mock the gods with prayer —
all they really ask is for us to be there

alert to their music, that is, their messages.
You'll hear it humming in your bones.
And your words too will learn to spin.

Swim, analyze the obvious
to find that mineral lode
within the shifting suchness all around.

The hard stuff, diamond in the rock,
mind in the meat.
Then watch them frolic in pure happenstance.

216.
The first thing I noticed
Stalinists are puritanical,
Christians have more fun with sex

even when not having it.
Everybody verbal, nobody smart —
the booksellers never opened a book

but still I stuck in that world
as long as I could,
doubts and conspiracies

and no mathematics to be done.
Just save a nickel to get home.
Now sixty years pass quickly and hello,

I'm home at last.
Forgive me for intruding, I just live here,
all the other voices are my own.

217.
Regrettable houses
curtains drawn
I walk alone

name me
by the food left uneaten on my plate
garnishes, vegetables, fuss.

But I walk with you,
I have been with you since hell
(you don't believe in hell)

and up the mountain
were we together,
linked sometimes by light alone

only our shadows mingling.
And now on this amniotic plain
the mists dispersing —

everyone is born
as one part of another,
we are always together,

your *own* other,
learn to listen to me
for I have paid,

deed all my nights to no one but you.
Hard as it is beautiful to be.
Agencies running through the ground —

don't you know who water *is*?
he asked, and at whose table
we are sustained? If light

becomes breath, from what
does water fall?
The old cosmologist was at his work again

bothering me with images.
I am too big for the world
he said, and silence seemed an answer

but who spoke that silence?
Do I have to be Irish to be wrong?
Blueberries from an Abnaki swamp,

sharks off Hilton Head, *Il Trovatore?*
Is that what people are these days,
shark bait and consumers?

Edel sei der Mensch !   he cried
using the imperative,
Human be noble, and scale the world

until every inch of it is known
and its blessing reckoned
and you have won its kiss.

So many voices told me this,
let belief fade into knowing,
then contemplate what is known,

the stuff inside the rose
that wins the hummingbird and brings the bee,
watch rapt in the mystery of nothing happening.

218.
Lady, did you see my fugue?
It ran this way,
it said it was finished and I believed it,

it took advantage of my credulity
and ran away, this way,
its nature to flee and mine to follow,

did you, Lady, hear my fugue?
It favors underbrush deep ravines,
hilltops, ruins, crowded streets,

it knows more names than it can touch,
it tries to wrap you in its changes
just to be being beautiful all over you

and you in it, illumining one another,
Lady, did you feel my fugue
nuzzling your sleepy ears,

growling in the engine of your car,
do you have a car, Lady,
will you take me with you where it goes,

rose at the end of the road?
I am too small for this world
the sunlight shames me and the *said*.

219.
Irritants in amber
sunbeams from another century
how quick the sea remembers us

I will not willingly live
in a place where no gull comes
white gliding with smooth hunger

even if they're rare,
midden heaps of Kingston
or right here sometimes.

Bridge over estuary and who knows?
Three percent saline at Rondout.
I need the near of it, the sometimes cry.

When all the flowers are on the tree
you can't tell which came first.
Read in any order, words wither soon enough.

Be ordinary, vague and pale
until you're stupid enough
to start singing — then beauty comes.

Angels explained this to Caedmon
who hardly listened
so loud was the music he found himself making.

220.
Exhaust the numbers
find the woman in the cave
smeared with red mud

river bottom, she presses
against cave wall
you are ripe with believing

you went down into the interior
to find her
the girl before language

you promise you'll be good to your mother
and write down the stories stones tell
you don't know if she believes you

or if she understands what you say
or even hears you.
It has grown dark outside

the trees are telling you something again
but you are like her,
lost in the maybes of hearing.

You reach out and touch her
since you are both alive
this is legitimate information

or is it? She seems
to be gone now. The wall
stands. And you are too.

I was as it happens alone in the cave,
my ochreous instructrix no longer where
anybody could get fingers red from touching her

was that what had been happening,
leaning on the wall, fondling granite?
A car door slams. Someone has come home.

221.
Little defilements
of milk and egg, glair
holds the image to itself,

I think we are defiled by what we see,
something happens to or in us
as in the old song you do

something to me. Solve.
No one can tell you
why anything happens,

leave it safe in algebra
a does some effect on *b* —
or *does* is too wrong a word.

Put *a* near *b* and something happens.
Is that all it ever means,
an ox walks by a house

and life changes forever?
Maybe syntax guides them
safely past the door,

she looks out the window wide enough,
but the animal is long gone,
the street is filled with doors

all of them seem closed faces.
Amor fati, fall in love with next door
no matter who lives there,

fall in love with the weather.
I can't forget how she said "I remember nothing"   *AT*
but that crow feather, luster-preening barbs

296

yesterday, where did I set it down?
sometimes we honor best by forgetting
how the woodchuck scurries safe beneath the porch

You gave me the feather
it came from the sky
a sign that the work was done.

222.
But a kid always wants the caboose,
to ride to the end of things,
a kid wants *All the way*!

be the last to get there,
have the clearest view
of where we've been.

Last days. I feel you love
we are only still beginning,
Eden in the rearview mirror

closer than it appears.
We are beginning.
Every archeologist knows we just woke up.

There seems a pressure in the air
that stifles the ears.
Crickets or tinnitus who can tell,

we are newborn all our days
immaturity is my sword and shield,
warm and humid today, must still be in the womb,

being born comes daily—
shake off the dream
or gird your loins with it —

so the words went by
like the mile- long freight train
no more meaning than a symphony —

it's nothing but time
some lover shaped
to happen to you

half an hour or so
carved
out of the silence in heaven.

223.
One more thing I have to tell you,
the sun was not always yellow,
she was deep red once, like blood,

but all our love and liturgy
was alchemy enough to turn her gold,
yellow as the secret camera of the rose.

224.
That's all, if any more happens
here I am.
Just call on me to recite

I'm in the infant school of language,
look, I raise my hand!
I won't know what to say until you call.

225.
Consider your image, Silence,
stone chipped away
to show some words inside

always words inside
always hard to read
to find in all the noise

the song it says.
And that's your image, Silence,
the delicate answer

catbird on the cable
triggering morning
can I trust him to remember

velocity of a sigh
heard over the phone—
where are you then, Silence,

when men and women imitate
what they think is you
by keeping still?

Can't you roar out at them then
overwhelm them
with the deep loud love you also are,

rich, earthy. ripeness?
When people don't answer one another
they need wet dirt beneath their feet,

feathers fallen, dust on the water glass.
True silence is friction
hot disclosure of something known

and that is why we have bodies
surely so we can share
the unique silence in each other.

226.
The morning was soft
there was so much more to be said
but it's not a lecture, it's a bird on a phone line

Desire is the difference
the blue side of the white stone
glows red in mindlight,

that's all the evening has to mark.
And it was morning as they said,
someday I'll believe them but not yet

too many angels for one message,
smell the bakers' oven and decide
"man is a chemical who laughs" he said

I didn't believe him either time
but we haven't gotten further than—
no names, please, we're still alive

twice I was a Christian
no matter what they said
I loved him because he is a door

he said, because he knew himself
better than I knew me,
when knowing is the same as being.

Enlightenment is not about light
it's about *ment*, the mind
behind light and anything else

so step out of the light into the light
where the darkness imagines you
I thought he said,

tried to work it out for myself,
the other party in this trinity
till we were one and none left over

I floundered in meanings
came away with salt on my lips
taste of the sea enough for one morning.

I ran my finger along the stone
trying to braille its history
or mine — this stone I give you

she had said, is you yourself,
fate, horoscope, analysis, stone.
Know it and you'll know yourself.

It's too big to fit in a pocket
too heavy to carry
I have to go to it each time

until by touch I find the answer
to that question I don't even know —
did she know it when she gave it,

or are we all just fingering rock somewhere
hoping something comes to mind
to tell us children what to do?

227.
There are no grown-ups in the real world
it's all hide-and-seek and playing house
and touching skin and crying in the night

we dream magazines to tell us otherwise,
to tell us our pain matters
and our hopes are shared, he laughed,

it's like a séance always
are the dead or living speaking
and how to tell them apart —

but I once saw an adult
he floated in the sky a while
and let me look at him as he rose

smaller and smaller till out of sight.
Any bird could tell me that
but I won't listen.

The small song
can only sing inside the long —
worship silence as your giving mother —

or as a caravan of carnivals
groveling across the deserts
hearing for you,

out loud the songs of vanished cities
all buried there, buried everywhere,
High Brazil and Margaretville —

the carnies ply their trade of loving you
with miracles of memory, weird animals,
dances you can't get out of mind.

Because mind is where they're born
and the desert only an excuse
for our brute restlessness —

always trust the paradox
sunrise with no sun
midnight bright around your heels.

228.
It was what I was waiting all my life to say,
the thing I didn't know I knew
and now he'd said it for me.

Count the leaves on that huge maple
and do them in proper order
then read the number and hear what it tells you

that's what music is doing while you sleep,
the horn call in Bruckner's 8th
announced the end of human time

learn to give each other with our hands.
Time is a solid now we only have
to shape and milk and feed each other with.

229.
And listened for an hour or so
to what they said,
took notes, rubbed his eyes,

went back to bed.
This is poetry.
This is the sky in which we live,

sleeping like swallows on the warmth
wells up from earth below us,
nothing disturbs the sleep of words.

I write from where I live
just like Sophocles or the man across the street.
But there is no street

so I have learned to listen to the trees
he said and I have learned
to hear him listening

as you hear me now
and will repeat all I said
with variations of your own

and call it all your own and it will be,
because no one speaks
except what he or she has heard —

any four-year old can tell you that.
Or Leiris and Bataille and Saussure
or that jogging woman with a fox at her side.

230.
The word is praying to itself
inside our words,
I am the temple

of the living god he said
and so are you.
Whatever exists is *for,*

for the sake of another
thing, one, house, heart,
mystery of all-day rain.

And I am the night
he said and it grew light,
child with a birthday toy.

The word prays to itself
in us — that's what I heard
when Janacek rolled out his harp

Our Father it sang   *Otce Nas*
to us who have only mothers
only one mother

so he needed voices to tell us
instruments and organ
but still we couldn't find him

we could only listen
and listening is beautiful,
the best mistake you can make.

231.
But begin with enigma
when leaves turn up their bellies in the wind
to quote your master he said

yourself when young.
It might rain — the sign
may become the signified,

the cows sprawl on the grass
to keep a space beneath them dry
your father said he said

sign and signified all at once
a bird meeting its own shadow
that's what the earth is good for,

a place where we can meet.
Make sense to me she said he said
I said we never stopped

and there is no beginning.
I've heard that before he said
but she was silent, smilent.

232.
Be arbitrary. Be anybody.
The world of capital
forgives every choice

just keep choosing.
Only the Hermit is villainous,
probably verminous,

disagreeable, old.
All the wrong things. He
of all men is not arbitrary.

He has chosen nothing
and nothing has accepted him
as her bride.

They live together
anywhere far away.
Sometimes I have dared to climb

the easier rock slopes of their abstruseness,
could even hear them talking from far off,
a man saying nothing with all his heart.

233.
One day he stood above me
firm on a lean cliff edge,
I called out to him Are you my mother?

He smiled and tossed me down a pear,
then drew back out of sight.
I ate it as I made my way down.

Where had he gotten such fruit?
Nothing grows on the rock.
How did he know he was my mother?

Satisfied, I did not come again.
The mountain is safe from me now
and I am as far from silence as before.

I know so little
I have made everything up
and it talks to me day and night

tries to persuade me it's the truth
but those who know don't tell.
So I paid scant attention to what I said.

You must be weary of my doubts
and of my certainties—in between's
a little Mohican stream of neither,

don't know where it comes from,
ripples past bright and clear
sometimes leaves crystals by our path.

It was here before anybody
and that's close enough to truth.
Many a time it's quenched my thirst

as long ago they think those crystals
cured the sicknesses of men and beasts,
tough transparent magic of compassion.

234.
Go back change
the beginning no beginning
leaf on no tree

a patch of whiteness
in shadow
shape of a heart

imagine me
so I can come again
into the forecourt

where the fountain lifts
and never falls
and the walls are only pictures

images strong enough
to keep invaders out
and cherish votaries,

humankind, the us.
No stone or steel required.
Place

takes care of itself
as a face guides you
to what the other person means

by being there
aloud.
Quick march to the riverside,

old men baptized again,
their mewling manners mended
like an old book

scotch tape on the pages
but the words clear
as muddled metaphor can be.

A bridge to nowhere!
Stagirite, explain myself,
in thy books I looked in vain

and so they closed my eyes on me
now I must write
what I cannot read

and all the stories start again
and never end.
Confession time. I have sinned

but not enough I think
if you can call that thinking
which peers through images at nothing at all.

235.
Mend us,
we don't know
when things end,

we still think this is music
or the American Republic
or my hand on your arm,

we get it wrong,
we go along,
and maybe it really is music —

do you hear me
when you close your eyes?
I see you when I close mine.

The sun is coming for me now
I see her through the trees,
she will take me from my doubts

into a yellow place she knows
and explain it all to me,
rivers and mountains, the real meaning of you.

236.
The sea in there
word boats bobbing dimly
far as the ear can see

maledetto, he cried,
you have soiled my sea
with saying.

And I grieved
to prove him right
but he was wrong.

The scum is always
the unsaid,
a word purifies itself in being spoken—

lift the sky off
just once to see
the imageless others

ourselves the sea.

3 June 2015 - 11 August 2015

CPSIA information can be obtained
at www.ICGtesting.com
Printed in the USA
FSHW021625231220
76864FS